THE PLEASURES OF tea

THE PLEASURES OF

Hearst Books

NEW YORK

tea

RECIPES & RITUALS

Text by Kim Waller
Foreword by Nancy Lindemeyer

It is the policy of William Morrow and Company, Inc., and its imprints and affiliates, recognizing the importance of preserving what has been written, to print the books we publish on acid-free paper, and we exert our best efforts to that end.

Library of Congress Cataloging-in-Publication Data
The pleasures of tea / by the editors of Victoria magazine.
    p.   cm.
   ISBN 0-688-16751-9
   1. Tea   2. Desserts   I. Victoria magazine (New York, N.Y.)
TX817.T3P72   1999   98-32092
641.3'372--DC21   CIP

Printed in Singapore

This book is set in Minion.

First Edition

10 9 8 7 6 5 4 3 2 1

www.williammorrow.com

For Victoria

Nancy Lindemeyer, *Editor-in-Chief*

Susan Maher, *Art Director*

John Mack Carter, *President,*
    Hearst Magazine Enterprises

Produced by Smallwood & Stewart, Inc.
New York City

Designer *Alexandra Maldonado*

Editor *Carrie Chase*

Contents

Tea Every Day 12

THROUGH THE DAY WITH TEA ∼ *Morning's First*

Cup, with recipes ∼ *Interview with a Tea Blender* ∼

Companionship of Tea, with recipes ∼ *Tea and a*

Good Book ∼ *The Comfort of Tea, with recipes*

Set for Tea   48

THE JOYS OF TEA COLLECTIONS ~ *The Collector's Cup ~ Wedgwood ~ The Glory of Chintz ~ A Tea Lover's Home ~ The Accoutrements of Tea ~ Visit a Tearoom, with recipes ~ Interview with a Tea Salon Owner*

Celebrations   82

TEA PARTIES FOR FRIENDS AND FAMILY ~ *For the Children, with recipes ~ Among Friends, with recipes ~ Interview with a Tea Grower ~ To Honor Love, with recipes ~ A Christmas Tea, with recipes*

Resources   122

Select Sources for Teas and Other Goods ~ Tea Salons ~ Tea Organizations, Tours, and Museums

TEA CAN STOP THE WORLD. IT HAS FOR ME FOR YEARS;

the British Empire, on which the sun never set, paused for tea daily. Tea, indeed,

can be regal and formal, but it is also simply a pleasure not to be denied. One of

Foreword

the most pleasant tea breaks I've ever had was on the set of a film. Nothing is

more hectic than movie production, but the producer and I sat in her office with

our mugs of tea and somehow held off the tension of ringing phones and frantic

assistants while we talked about the books we loved when we were growing up.

Each of us has the privilege of our own tea ritual. I know tea lovers are

keen to have the proper setting, the right time of day, the carefully selected book

at the ready. And let us not forget our tea friends. What better excuse to get

together in informal ways? Tea also inspires us to create tasty treats for our own

quiet moments or special gatherings. I am amazed how varied the fare can be.

So please come to the pleasures of tea with the great expectation of delight.

⁓ Nancy Lindemeyer

THERE'S HARDLY AN OCCASION THAT DOES NOT SEEM

just right for tea ⁓ from a neighbor at the door to a festive bridal shower

to a rainy afternoon with the grandchildren. And for each of these occasions

Introduction

there is such a variety of teas, and so many exquisitely beautiful teacups and

pots, that deciding on your favorites can be an adventure in itself. This

book invites you to explore the many moods of tea, whether solitary or cel-

ebratory. You'll find party ideas that relax host and guests alike, collectibles

and decorating ideas for tea lovers, tips and lore, and, of course, a wealth of

mouthwatering recipes both sweet and savory that will become a cherished

part of your repertoire. Teatime, anytime, is a delicious ceremony of friend-

ship and sharing. So put on the kettle ⁓ it's time for tea!

Tea Every Day

Tea is a daily companion that never fails us. It warms when we ～ or the world ～ feel cold, gives strength when we're weary, and lends delicious grace notes to our gatherings. From the first cheery chortle of the kettle at dawn, to the fragrance of an evening cup as the house quiets and we turn to our reading, tea can be counted on to smooth and save the day.

BREW A CUP; BREW A DAY. UNHURRIEDLY.

The sunrise song of tea is lyrical, but with bracing undertones. "Of course you can," it murmurs encouragingly. The flavor holds a hint of far lands,

Morning's First Cup

yet is as familiar as the cat that comes rubbing or sunlight on the window sill. And as you lift your first cup of tea and feel its warmth, the day's challenges settle into perspective. A breakfast tea implies breakfast ⁓ an important meal we're often tempted to scant or rush through. Those hearty, homey smells of breakfast filling the kitchen are part of morning's joy and childhood's memories, whether of homemade English muffins to slather with jam or simply a bit of sugared cinnamon gilding the toast. When you take the time to fortify yourself or your family with something special like blueberry fritters, you are

⁓ Can every day hold a bit of Sunday? Not always, but when you or a loved one are about to depart on a trip (or have just returned from one), a tasty breakfast with tea beautifully served at bedside restores both body and spirit.

Tea blends with hearty wake-up notes, such as English and Irish breakfast teas, lend courage to the morning. Usually a mix of Ceylon and Assam, often with Darjeeling, these teas stand up well to a splash of milk.

making a sovereign statement: This part of the day is about us.

To emphasize the point, indulge the eye as well as the taste buds. A bedside repast with fresh flowers on a lace-lined tray (and never mind the inevitable crumbs on the quilt) is not for newlyweds alone: Try it midlife, before the most stressful of working days.

For some people, starting the day means wrapping hands around a favorite sturdy mug; others see no reason to reserve the beauty of an antique cup just for guests. Whichever you might choose, there's a ritualistic comfort in using pretty objects you love that no impersonal carton from the corner deli can impart. (Moreover, cardboard and styrofoam are inimical to tea's subtle flavors.)

As you infuse your morning with the invigorating aroma of tea, you are taking a brief, quiet stand against the utilitarian world. These moments belong to serenity.

A Tea Blender

In the colonial New England village of Salisbury, Connecticut, John Harney and his sons Michael and Paul purvey a dazzling spectrum of the world's high-quality teas to luxury hotels and tea lovers across the land. "How many teas do we taste each year? In the thousands," says Michael Harney. "My dad, John, learned about tea from an English mentor, then started our company in 1983 with the idea of providing the best-quality teas available. He felt that the more people could experience really fine teas, the more they would demand them; and that's proved true." Today you'll find well over 125 teas and blends ∼ from four Earl Greys, twenty green teas, and First and Second Flush Darjeelings to herbal, organic, and decaffeinated teas ∼ all fascinatingly described in Harney & Sons'

catalog. As the main buyer now, Michael has journeyed to India, Ceylon, Japan, and China, where the tender leaves are plucked by hand. "Unlike wine, which is harvested once a year, the tea of a single tea garden may give you 200 pickings to buy, each varying according to season and weather conditions," says Michael. "You're not just buying a product, but a moment of that product." Growers or brokers send samples to Salisbury, and decisions must be made quickly. Forty percent of Harney's teas are their own blends ∼ including delicious concoctions like their chocolate mint tea ("wonderful after dinner") and Paul Harney's new line of organic teas. "People today are far more willing to try fine teas, different teas," says Michael ∼ surely thanks, in part, to Harney & Sons.

Orange pekoe tea, a flowery, favorite morning blend, has nothing to do with oranges. To suggest an elegant tea, Dutch traders named it for the princes of the House of Orange; today it refers to the size of the leaf picked.

English Muffins

English muffin purists insist that you should never slice open a muffin to toast it. Instead, cut a sliver in the side and toast whole. When done, poke butter in through the slit and savor the muffin with your morning cup.

¼ cup warm (110°F) water
Pinch of sugar
1 envelope active dry yeast
1½ cups warm (110°F) milk
2 tablespoons unsalted butter, cut into
   bits and softened
1 tablespoon honey
About 5¼ cups all-purpose flour
1¼ teaspoons salt
Cornmeal

1. In a small bowl, combine the warm water and sugar. Sprinkle the yeast over the top and let stand until the yeast dissolves and becomes foamy, about 10 minutes.

2. Meanwhile, butter the large bowl of an electric mixer. Combine the milk, butter, and honey in the bowl and stir until the butter is almost melted.

3. Stir in 2½ cups flour and the yeast mixture. Beat at high speed for 3 minutes, or until well combined. Cover the dough with a tea towel and let it rise in a warm place, away from drafts, until it is doubled in volume, about 30 minutes.

4. Butter a 4-quart mixing bowl and set aside. Stir the salt into the dough. With a wooden spoon stir in enough of the remaining flour so the dough forms a ball.

5. Turn the dough out onto a well-floured surface. Knead the dough until it is smooth and elastic, about 8 to 10 minutes, adding enough of the remaining flour to keep the dough from sticking. Transfer the dough to the prepared bowl, turning it once to coat the top of the dough with butter.

6. Cover the dough with a tea towel and let it rise in a warm place, away from drafts, until it is doubled in volume, about 45 minutes.

7. Punch the dough down and divide it in half. Sprinkle a bread board generously with the cornmeal. Place half the dough on the board and sprinkle more cornmeal over the top of the dough.

8. Gently roll the dough out into a ½-inch-thick round. Cut out the English muffins with a floured 3-inch biscuit cutter. Repeat with the remaining dough. Arrange the dough rounds 2 inches apart on ungreased baking sheets. Knead, reroll, and cut the dough scraps once, if desired.

9. Cover the muffins with a tea towel and let them rise in a warm place, away from drafts, until they are doubled in volume, about 30 minutes.

10. Heat a lightly oiled nonstick griddle or skillet over medium-high heat. Lift some of the dough rounds with a spatula onto the griddle. Cook for 2 minutes on each side, then reduce the heat to medium and cook, turning every few minutes, for 13 to 18 minutes, until done in the center.

11. Cool the muffins on wire racks while you cook the remaining muffins.

Makes: 10 to 12 muffins

Strawberry–Lemon Balm Butter

Even ordinary toast and pancakes perk up with this special butter, a perfect recipe for kitchen gardeners: Lemon balm and strawberries are both ready for picking in June.

1 cup (2 sticks) softened unsalted butter
3 tablespoons confectioners' sugar, or
    more to taste
⅓ cup finely chopped strawberries
2 tablespoons chopped fresh lemon balm

1. In a food processor, combine the butter and confectioners' sugar. Process until the mixture is creamy.

2. Add the strawberries and lemon balm. Pulse just until the mixture is well combined. (If the strawberries are particularly tart, add another tablespoon of confectioners' sugar.)

3. Transfer the butter to a small bowl, cover with plastic wrap, and refrigerate until ready to serve.

Makes: about 1⅓ cups

Spicy Rose Tea

If you don't have pesticide-free rose petals handy, substitute pesticide-free lavender flowers, borage flowers, or sweet violets for an equally fragrant, eye-opening blend.

1 tablespoon fresh pesticide-free
    rose petals or 1 teaspoon dried
4 teaspoons orange pekoe tea
½ teaspoon cinnamon stick chips

1. Pour boiling water into the teapot and set aside for 5 minutes. Discard the water.

2. Gently crush the rose petals to release their flavor. Put them into a tea ball along with the tea and cinnamon chips. Cover the tea ball and place in the teapot. Cover with boiling water and let steep for 5 minutes.

3. Remove the tea ball from the teapot and discard the solids. Serve the tea immediately.

Makes: 4 to 6 servings

Cinnamon-Raisin Bread

For an intriguing twist on this swirly bread, soak the raisins in black tea, then drain well before adding them to the batter. When choosing foods for a breakfast menu, bear in mind that anything with spice stands up to robust black teas like Ceylon, orange pekoe, and Darjeeling.

RAISIN DOUGH

> ¼ cup warm (110°F) water
>
> 3 tablespoons sugar, plus a pinch
>
> 1 envelope active dry yeast
>
> 3 tablespoons unsalted butter, cut into bits
>
> 1½ teaspoons salt
>
> 2 cups warm (110°F) milk
>
> 6½ to 7 cups all-purpose flour
>
> ½ cup dark raisins
>
> ½ cup golden raisins

CINNAMON FILLING

> ½ cup sugar
>
> 1 tablespoon ground cinnamon

TO MAKE THE RAISIN DOUGH

1. Butter two 9- by 5- by 3-inch loaf pans. Butter a 4-quart bowl. Set aside.

2. In a small bowl, combine the warm water and the pinch of sugar. Sprinkle the yeast over the top and let stand until the yeast dissolves and becomes foamy, about 10 minutes.

3. Meanwhile, in the large bowl of an electric mixer, combine the remaining 3 table-spoons sugar, the butter, and salt. Pour in the warm milk. Stir until the butter is almost melted.

4. Stir in 3 cups flour and the yeast mixture.

Beat at high speed for 3 minutes. With a wooden spoon, stir in the raisins, then stir in enough of the remaining flour so the dough forms a ball.

5. Turn the dough out onto a well-floured surface, and knead the dough until it is smooth and elastic, 8 to 10 minutes, adding enough of the remaining flour to keep the dough from sticking. Place the dough in the prepared bowl, turning it once to coat the top of the dough with butter.

6. Cover the dough with a tea towel and let it rise in a warm place, away from drafts, until it is doubled in volume, 1¼ to 1½ hours.

7. Punch the dough down. Turn it out onto a well-floured surface, and divide it in half. Cover the dough with a tea towel and let it rest for about 10 minutes.

TO MAKE THE CINNAMON FILLING

8. Meanwhile, in a small bowl, combine the sugar and cinnamon.

9. Roll half the dough into a 12- by 8-inch rectangle. Sprinkle with half the cinnamon filling. Press the filling into the dough.

10. Starting at a short side, roll the dough up tightly, jelly-roll fashion. Pinch the dough together at the seam. Pinch the ends to seal and fold under the loaf. Place seam side down in a prepared loaf pan. Repeat with the remaining dough.

11. Cover the dough with a tea towel and let it rise in a warm place, away from drafts, until it is doubled in volume, 45 to 60 minutes.

12. Preheat the oven to 375°F.

13. Bake the loaves for 40 to 45 minutes. Tent the pans loosely with aluminum foil during the last 15 minutes to prevent overbrowning.

14. Remove the loaves from the pans and cool slightly on wire racks.

Makes: 2 loaves

Blueberry Fritters

These crisp fritters must be served as soon as they are cooked. The temperature of the frying oil is crucial, so be sure to allow it to reheat between batches.

> Oil, for deep-frying
> 1 cup all-purpose flour
> ¼ cup granulated sugar
> 1¼ teaspoons baking powder
> ½ teaspoon salt
> ¼ teaspoon ground cinnamon
> ¼ teaspoon ground nutmeg
> ¼ teaspoon ground allspice
> 2 large eggs, separated
> 1 tablespoon fresh lemon juice
> 1 teaspoon vegetable oil
> ⅓ cup milk
> ½ cup dried blueberries
> Confectioners' sugar, for garnish

1. In a deep fryer, heat the oil to 375°F. In a medium-size bowl, combine the flour, granulated sugar, baking powder, salt, cinnamon, nutmeg, and allspice; mix well and set aside.

2. In the large bowl of an electric mixer, at medium speed, beat the egg yolks with the lemon juice and 1 teaspoon oil until well combined. Beat in the milk until just blended. Gradually add the flour mixture, beating until smooth. Set aside.

3. Wash the beaters. In the clean dry small bowl of the electric mixer, at high speed, beat the egg whites until they are stiff. Fold the whites into the batter. Gently fold in the blueberries.

4. Preheat the oven to 200°F. Drop 2 or 3 large spoonfuls of batter into the hot oil and cook, turning occasionally, until the fritters are puffed and the outside is crisp and brown, about 5 minutes. (Do not undercook. The fritters will brown quickly at first but need additional cooking for the centers to cook and puff up.) Remove the fritters from the oil with a slotted spoon and drain on a paper towel–lined plate. Transfer the fritters to an ungreased baking sheet and keep warm in the oven. Repeat with the remaining batter.

5. Sift the confectioners' sugar over the fritters. Transfer the fritters to a serving plate and serve immediately.

Makes: 10 to 12 fritters

> Queen Victoria was the first to drop a slice of lemon into an English teacup. She tried it while visiting her married daughter in Germany ⁓ and loved it!

for a tea break is a good one. A friend at the door, shopping accomplished, or a task that's stuck ~ the occasion definitely calls for sitting down with

Companionship of Tea

a nice cup of tea. If you're working at home, relax in another room entirely (preferably at a decent remove from the telephone) in a corner devoted to comfort alone. Too often, our afternoon speeds up just as we're slowing down, feeling a bit low on ideas and blood sugar, so the time-honored tradition of afternoon tea with a bite of something delicious has a sound biological basis.

A spot of tea is always a spot of calm. Try it as the cure for a meeting that's going nowhere, and watch everyone loosen up around an attractive tray of brownies, lemon slices, and steaming Earl Grey. As spoons clink, smiles return. Indeed,

~ Between sips, conversation brightens, confidences flow. Flavored blends, flowery Jasmine, or citrusy Earl Grey (which is tossed while drying with bergamot) have the gold of the afternoon in them. Or compliment your guests with Darjeeling, considered by many to be the queen of teas.

in some countries, no business arrangement is discussed or confirmed without tea, a universal gesture of hospitality that expresses our urge for unity. It's hard not to be affable over tea.

My hour for tea is half-past five, and my buttered toast waits for nobody.

~ Wilkie Collins, *The Woman in White*

For the custom of afternoon tea, we have a peckish English duchess to thank. In the early nineteenth century, Anna, the Duchess of Bedford, experienced a "sinking feeling" at about four, several hours before dinnertime. Not wishing to bestir her staff, she requested just a cup of tea with a slice of cake. Soon friends were joining her for this late afternoon delight, and the ritual spread, becoming an elaborate social gathering well sweetened with jam tarts, pastries, and even little sandwiches. (We err when we call this event "high tea," for that was the English working man's hearty six o'clock supper.) Today, as the afternoon sun slants, we might well raise a cup to the hungry Duchess.

Tea and a Good Book

There is no better company than tea when you settle down
to read of other times, other lives, and find yourself there.

Pilgrim at Tinker Creek, Annie Dillard
Essays that plumb nature and the spirit

The Transit of Venus, Shirley Hazzard
The entwined life journeys of two orphaned sisters

Corelli's Mandolin, Louis de Bernieres
Courage and compassion on a modern Greek island

To the Lighthouse, Virginia Woolf
Mrs. Ramsay's household, Woolf's masterpiece

Tell Me a Story, Tillie Olsen
Three stories that unfold the depths in women's daily lives

Cold Mountain, Charles Frazier
A soldier and his beloved in Civil War America

Rebecca, Daphne du Maurier
A second wife haunted by the mystery of the first

Lark Rise to Candleford, Flora Thompson
The postmistress's view of English village life

Tender Is the Night, F. Scott Fitzgerald
Cavorting on the French Riviera in the 1920s

Possession, A.S. Byatt
A Victorian poet's romance, uncovered by a scholar

The Selected Poems of Emily Dickinson
Poems forever fresh that search the soul

OTHER USES FOR TEA

TEA-DYE linen fabrics (right) or tired-looking white cottons and prints: blouses, drapes, nightgowns. A mixture of black tea and plum tea gives a soft pinkish cast.

CREATE "ANTIQUE" DOCUMENTS or a treasure-hunt map. Roughly tear the edges of a firm white paper, crinkle it up, then spread it out. Run a hot tea bag over the paper, blotching here and there. If the look is not aged enough, let the paper dry, then blotch again.

SOOTHE sunburn or bee stings with a chilled used tea bag or used leaves. This is also an excellent poultice for puffy or tired eyes.

FOR A FACIAL, put plenty of chamomile tea and hot water in a large bowl. When the steam is safe, bend over the bowl, your head tented by a towel, and feel the steam open your pores.

GIVE YOUR PLANTS A BOOST by treating them to your leftover tea. Mix used leaves (not the bag) into houseplant or garden soil. Roses love it!

On a hot summer afternoon, nothing quenches thirst like a green tea. Some well-known green teas include the refreshing Gunpowder and the more mellow Dragonwell, one of China's most celebrated. Powdered green tea leaves also bring fresh fragrance to homemade soaps.

Tomato and Goat Cheese Sandwiches

When you slice open an heirloom tomato, you can actually smell the sweetness from the next room. Not available at supermarkets, these old-fashioned varieties are sometimes featured at farmstands or in specialty catalogs. The touch of tarragon acts as a flavor bridge to the Iced Lemon Balm Tea, as the herb's subtle anise taste enhances both tomatoes and lemons.

> ¼ cup balsamic vinegar
> 2 to 4 small different-color ripe heirloom tomatoes
> 4 ounces fresh goat cheese
> 1 tablespoon snipped fresh chives
> 1 teaspoon minced fresh tarragon
> ½ teaspoon freshly ground black pepper
> Two 4- by 4-inch slices bread, such as focaccia, cut ¼ inch thick
> Salt, to taste
> 1 tablespoon olive oil
> 4 sprigs tarragon, for garnish

1. In a small saucepan, bring the balsamic vinegar to a boil and cook until reduced by two thirds. Set aside to cool.

2. Thinly slice the tomatoes. Transfer them to a paper towel–lined plate to drain.

3. In a small bowl, combine the goat cheese, chives, minced tarragon, and ¼ teaspoon pepper and blend well.

4. Spread half of the cheese mixture on one slice of the bread, top with the remaining slice of bread, and spread with the remaining cheese mixture. Arrange the slices of tomatoes on the top of the cheese mixture,

overlapping them. Sprinkle the tomatoes with salt and the remaining ¼ teaspoon pepper and drizzle with the oil and vinegar.

5. To serve, cut the sandwich into four pieces and garnish each with a sprig of tarragon.

Makes: 4 sandwiches

Iced Lemon Balm Tea

Lemon balm naturally has a hint of mint and lemon, but we've intensified the flavors by adding the real things. Just as lemon and mint cleanse the palate, this tea acts as a graceful transition from scones to tarts to sandwiches on an afternoon menu. You'll never miss the caffeine, either: The tea's uplifting aroma is invigorating enough.

> 1 bunch (1½ to 2 ounces) fresh lemon balm
> 1 small lemon, thinly sliced
> 4 mint tea bags
> 3 tablespoons honey

1. Reserve 6 sprigs of the lemon balm for garnish. Combine the remaining lemon balm, the lemon slices, and tea bags in a teapot or bowl. Pour in about 2 cups

boiling water to cover. Cover and let steep for 5 minutes.

2. Remove and discard the tea bags. Stir the honey into the tea and set aside to cool to room temperature.

3. Strain the tea through a fine-meshed sieve into a large pitcher and discard the solids. Add 4 cups cold water and stir well. Refrigerate the tea until serving time.

4. Pour the chilled tea over ice in glasses. Garnish with the reserved lemon balm.

Makes: 6 servings

Cranberry-Orange Conserve

A conserve, a mixture of at least two fruits cooked with sugar, makes a fine spread for scones and muffins, a topping for ice cream, or a cake filling.

> 1 (12-ounce) package fresh or frozen cranberries
> 1 navel orange, coarsely chopped (including peel)
> ¾ cup sugar
> 1 cup water
> ½ cup toasted slivered almonds

1. In a large nonreactive saucepan, combine the cranberries, orange, sugar, and water. Bring the mixture to a boil, stirring to dissolve the sugar. Reduce the heat and simmer, stirring occasionally, for 5 to 7 minutes, until the cranberries pop.

2. Remove the saucepan from the heat and stir in the almonds. Spoon into a serving bowl.

Makes: 3½ cups

Raisin and Nut Scones

Although inspired by Dundee cake, that fruity Irish delicacy made with raisins and nuts, these scones are far easier to prepare and not as filling ⁓ afternoon tea is, after all, a respite, not a meal. Clotted cream, if available, and strawberry jam are ideal toppings.

> 2 cups all-purpose flour
> ¼ cup sugar
> 4 teaspoons baking powder
> 5 tablespoons cold unsalted butter, cut into bits
> ¼ cup half-and-half
> 2 large eggs, lightly beaten
> ½ cup chopped mixed nuts
> ¼ cup dark raisins

1. Butter a baking sheet. Sift the flour, sugar, and baking powder into a large bowl. Add the butter and blend until the mixture resembles a coarse meal. In a small bowl, beat together the half-and-half and eggs. Stir the egg mixture into the flour mixture until just combined. Add the nuts and raisins and stir until a dough forms.

2. Turn the dough out onto a lightly floured surface and pat the dough into a ⅓-inch-thick round. With a 2½-inch floured cutter, cut out rounds. Arrange the rounds 2 inches apart on the prepared baking sheet. Let stand for 20 minutes.

3. Preheat the oven to 400°F.

4. Bake the scones for 15 to 20 minutes, until lightly golden.

Makes: about 12 scones

Poppy Seed–Jam Tarts

Scandinavian in origin, these little tarts are a study in contrasts: delightfully crunchy poppy seeds against silky jam. If you prefer tarts without icing, just top with whipped cream right before serving.

POPPY SEED–JAM TARTS

1 cup (2 sticks) unsalted butter, softened
½ cup granulated sugar
1 large egg yolk
1 teaspoon vanilla extract
3 tablespoons poppy seeds
2½ to 2¾ cups all-purpose flour
1 cup very thick strawberry and/or
    apricot jam

ICING

1 cup confectioners' sugar
About 2 tablespoons heavy cream

TO MAKE THE POPPY SEED–JAM TARTS

1. Line a baking sheet with plastic wrap. In the large bowl of an electric mixer, at medium speed, beat the butter and granulated sugar until light and fluffy. Add the egg yolk and vanilla and continue beating until the mixture is well combined.

2. Reduce the mixer speed to low and add the poppy seeds. Gradually beat in enough of the flour to make a moderately stiff dough. Spread the dough into a 6-inch square on the prepared baking sheet and wrap it in the plastic wrap. Refrigerate the dough for at least 2 hours, or overnight.

3. Preheat the oven to 375°F. Spray sixteen 2¾- by 1-inch-deep tartlet pans with nonstick cooking spray and place on a baking sheet.

4. Cut the dough into 16 equal pieces. Roll each piece into a ball. Using your fingers, press the balls into rounds, then gently press into the prepared tartlet pans, leaving an indentation in the center of the tarts for the filling. Fill each center with 1 tablespoon of the jam.

5. Bake for 12 to 15 minutes, until the edges are golden brown. Cool in the pans on wire racks. Carefully remove the tarts from the pans.

TO MAKE THE ICING

6. In a small bowl, stir together the confectioners' sugar and just enough cream to reach a piping consistency.

7. Put the icing into a pastry bag fitted with a number 1 tip. Randomly pipe a lacy pattern of icing on the tarts. Place the tarts on a serving plate and serve.

Makes: 16 tarts

Citrus-Flavored Honey

Flavored honeys are easy to make and brighten up the morning's cup of tea or muffin.

1 (16-ounce) jar light unflavored honey
Zest of 2 lemons or oranges, cut into spirals

1. In a small saucepan, stir the honey over medium heat until it is warmed through.

2. Place the zest in a heat-proof jar. Pour in the warmed honey. Cool to room temperature.

3. Cover tightly and let stand for at least 1 week before using.

Makes: 1½ cups

SUPPER IS OVER, THE FIRE LIT, THE book awaiting. In the hours before bedtime, in Jane Austen's day, tea was an evening pleasure taken in the parlor as the family played cards or

The Comfort of Tea

sewed and chatted. Today, when a circle of friends gather of an evening to knit, or to discuss books or investments, it's tea, sipped slowly and poured frequently, that best floats the conversation. There are many answers to what we ask of an evening's cup, but mostly that it quiet the spirit and settle the stomach, that it relax and ease us toward sleep filled with a sense of well-being.

Tea has been considered an aid to meditation since it was first drunk in China. In Japan, its ceremonial preparation is an art form that focuses and cleanses the spirit. Let a quiet evening cup be your guide to new, long thoughts.

Though India teas have the reputation of being "athletic," teas from China, which first came to England through Holland, are considered more "reflective." Among them, lettuce-pale green tea, whose fresh leaves are dried quickly (arresting the

process of fermentation that gives us black teas), is not only wonderful as a palate-cleanser with food, but has gained new popularity in the West because its antioxidant qualities promote health and longevity. It's a delicate sip, which needs no milk or sweeteners; or, if you prefer a touch of sweetness, try Passion Fruit Sencha.

Although tea has about 60 percent less caffeine than coffee, it does have some. Those who wish their life ⁓ or just their evenings ⁓ to be caffeine-free are among the legions who love exploring herbal and fruit teas, not least for their intriguing range of delicious flavors. Evening's most soothing teas invariably include chamomile, made from the daisy-like flower, not the leaf, of the plant. The very word (say it slowly) tastes like peace, and that is its gift. Mint, too, especially spearmint, has a relaxing and digestive effect; and for a queasy stomach, ginger tea is marvelous.

What could be more soothing when one is down with a virus than hot tea laced with honey and lemon? Apparently, drinking tea benefits us well or ill: The polyphenols and essential oils help lower cholesterol, the caffeine stimulates digestion, and green tea contains vitamin C.

Herbal infusions, also known as tisanes, have a long medicinal history in both the East and the West. Many of Europe's Renaissance gardens, in fact, such as the enduringly lovely Chelsea Physic Garden in London, were initially devoted to healing plants, whose salubrious powers were often ingested as teas. An infinity of tasty plants have found their way back to the teacup, to be inventively blended with everything from blackberry leaves and rose hips to lemon balm and alfalfa leaves. Dried apples, plums, or citrus peels are also zesty, popular additions, along with spices such as cinnamon or vanilla. Gone are the days when Constant Comment, that orangey old favorite, was the only choice for those who craved intense flavors in a cup!

These days, every gardener is something of an herbalist. Try drying your own pesticide-free garden herbs (completely, so no moisture remains) and launch on the adventure of creating your signature house blends!

Rhubarb and Ginger Jam

What a nice treat to have on hand ⁓ perfect for spreading over a simple late-night dessert of gingerbread or pound cake. You might also find yourself spreading this on toast the next morning.

> 4 pounds trimmed rhubarb, cut into 1-inch pieces (14 cups)
> 6¾ cups sugar
> 2 teaspoons ground ginger
> ½ teaspoon citric acid (available at pharmacies)

1. In a heavy-bottomed 8-quart nonreactive Dutch oven, layer the rhubarb alternately with the sugar. Cover tightly and let stand in a cool place for 24 hours.

2. Stir in the ginger and citric acid. Bring the mixture to a boil over high heat, stirring to dissolve the sugar. Reduce the heat slightly but continue to boil rapidly, stirring often to prevent sticking, about 25 to 30 minutes; until the mixture is very thick, the jam should "sheet" off the spoon when it is lifted. Remove the pan from the heat; stir gently and skim off the foam.

3. Ladle the jam into 8 hot sterilized half-pint canning jars, leaving ¼ inch of headspace. Seal the jars according to the manufacturer's directions. Place the jars in a boiling water bath and process for 5 minutes after the water returns to a boil. (Add 1 minute for each 1,000 feet above sea level.)

4. Cool the jars on a wire rack. Store them in a cool dry dark place.

Makes: 8 half-pints

Orange-Marmalade Cake

Real orange syrup locked into the buttermilk-rich layers tenderizes this homespun cake. Though the Soothing Tea perfectly complements this light, citrusy dessert, any mild green tea would also suit, or even a first-flush Darjeeling such as Mim, a delicate spring harvest tea with a hint of white grapes and a flowery aroma.

ORANGE CAKE

> 3 cups cake flour
> ½ teaspoon baking soda
> ½ teaspoon salt
> 1 cup (2 sticks) softened unsalted butter
> 2 cups sugar
> 3 large eggs, at room temperature, lightly beaten
> 1 tablespoon grated orange zest
> 1½ teaspoons vanilla extract
> 1 cup buttermilk, at room temperature

ORANGE SYRUP

> 1 cup fresh orange juice
> ¼ cup sugar

MARMALADE FILLING

> 1 cup orange marmalade

SOUR CREAM FROSTING

> ¾ cup well-chilled heavy cream
> 3 tablespoons sugar
> ¾ cup well-chilled sour cream

TO MAKE THE ORANGE CAKE

1. Preheat the oven to 325°F. Butter two 9-inch round cake pans, line them with parchment paper, and butter and flour the paper, shaking out the excess.

2. Sift together the flour, baking soda, and salt into a large bowl.

Victoria fair

Our Festive Chintzware Collection

We are thrilled to offer you a new heirloom, our chintzware collection in the "Welbeck" pattern, out of production since the 1960's, but made for us in Straffordshire, England. Royal Winton, the century-old company that in 1934 first introduced "Welbeck," with its happy profusion of roses, daffodils, tulips, and wisteria, has created this collection of earthenware for us.

Our six-cup teapot in the "Ascot" shape, with pattern-covered spout and handle, is a truly attractive collectible.

Chintz has become highly collectible and scarce - making this a rare opportunity indeed to acquire this enchanting china. Give them to a bride, yourself — indeed, anyone who appreciates fine tableware!

See other side for new items

RIBBON NOT INCLUDED

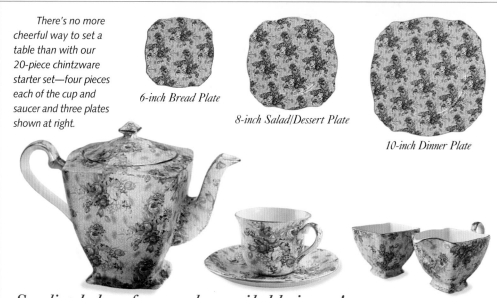

There's no more cheerful way to set a table than with our 20-piece chintzware starter set—four pieces each of the cup and saucer and three plates shown at right.

6-inch Bread Plate

8-inch Salad/Dessert Plate

10-inch Dinner Plate

See list below for newly available items!

To order call 1-800-223-3089 and ask for Dept. VI081 .

Or indicate your selections below and send with your check or money order to:

**Department VI081, P. O. Box 7765
Red Oak, IA 51591-0765**

___#302533 Chintzware teapot $150.00

___#302535 Chintzware creamer and sugar set $80.00

___#302594 Chintzware cup and saucer $195.00/set of 4

___#302792 20-Piece Chintzware starter set, $605.00

___#302538 Chintzware dinner plates $165.00/set of 4

___#302537 Chintzware salad/dessert plates

$135.00/set of 4

___#302749 Chintzware bread plates $110.00/set of 4

___#302759 Chintzware bell 3¼" high $29.95

___#302775 Chintzware bells $85.95/set of 3

New Chintzware Items *(not shown)*

___#302667 Rim Soups 7" dia. $120.00/set of 4

___#302750 18" Platter $130.00

___#302751 Cake Comport 10¾"dia., 5"h $125.00

___#302753 Sauce Boat w/ Tray 8oz. $110.00

1-800-223-3089

Shipping and Handling Charges

Under $30	$ 4.95
$30 to $49.99	$ 5.95
$50 to $74.99	$ 6.95
$75 to $149.99	$ 8.95
$150 to $199.99	$ 9.95
$200 and over	$12.95

Billing Address:

Name
Please Print

Address

City   *State*   *Zip*

Daytime Phone

V1081

3. In the large bowl of an electric mixer, at medium-high speed, beat the butter until creamy. Add the sugar a little at a time and beat the mixture until light and fluffy. Beat in the eggs, orange zest, and vanilla. Add the flour, alternately with the buttermilk in three additions, beating after each addition just until smooth.

4. Divide the batter between the prepared pans, smoothing the surface, and rap each pan on the counter to burst any air pockets. Bake for 45 minutes, or until a toothpick inserted in the center comes out clean. Transfer the cakes to wire racks to cool for 20 minutes.

TO MAKE THE ORANGE SYRUP

5. Meanwhile, in a medium-size bowl, stir together the orange juice and sugar until the sugar is dissolved.

6. With a toothpick, poke holes at $\frac{1}{2}$-inch intervals in the cake layers. Gradually spoon the syrup over the layers, allowing each addition to be completely absorbed before adding more syrup. Let the layers cool completely.

TO MAKE THE MARMALADE FILLING

7. In a small saucepan over medium heat, heat the marmalade until just melted. Set aside to cool for 5 minutes.

TO MAKE THE SOUR CREAM FROSTING

8. In a medium-size bowl, whisk the heavy cream with the sugar until it forms firm peaks. Add the sour cream a little at a time and whisk until the frosting resembles a spreadable consistency.

9. Invert one of the layers onto a cake plate and carefully peel off the parchment paper. Spread two thirds of the marmalade filling over the top, smoothing it evenly. Invert the remaining cake layer onto the top of the first one and peel off the parchment paper. Spoon the remaining marmalade onto the top, leaving a $1\frac{1}{4}$-inch border around the edge. Frost the sides of the cake and the border with the sour cream frosting, leaving the marmalade exposed. Chill for at least 2 hours before serving.

Makes: 10 to 12 servings

Soothing Tea

Linden leaves and flowers (sometimes called basswood or lime) are legendary for calming the nerves and promoting restful sleep.

> 1 tablespoon pesticide-free linden leaves and flowers
> 1 tablespoon pesticide-free chamomile
> 1 tablespoon fragrant pesticide-free rose petals

1. Pour boiling water into the teapot and set aside for 5 minutes. Discard the water.

2. Gently crush the linden leaves and flowers, chamomile and rose petals to release their flavor. Put them into a tea ball, cover the tea ball and place in the teapot. Cover with boiling water and let steep for 5 minutes.

3. Remove the tea ball from the teapot. Serve the tea immediately.

Makes: 4 to 6 servings

Set for Tea

The sheer artistry that shines from tea things ~ from silver sugar tongs to shell-thin porcelain cups ~ is a testament to tea's value in our lives. Just looking at them brings a message of comfort and welcome. And with every pretty cup or pot we collect, new or antique, we draw pleasure from a long tradition linking beauty and grace with the taking of tea.

WHAT TURNS A DRINK OF TEA INTO AN occasion? Often, the cup it is served in ∼ no doubt one reason why so many tea lovers are just as devoted to lovely china as they are to their orange

The Collector's Cup

pekoe or lapsang souchong. Collecting can start with the jog of a childhood memory ∼ perhaps a swirl of rosebuds recalls some long-ago cup in which an adored grandmother offered you a bit of sweet, milky tea scented with cinnamon. Soon you're haunting flea markets or scanning the shelves of antiques shops for others of its style or pattern. And the rarer and finer the pattern, the more exciting the hunt.

There are many individual ways to build a collection you'll love to display, use, and share with friends. One casual collector never passes up a nice teacup patterned with pansies, new or old (or an

∼ When kaolin, the fine white clay from which porcelain is made, was discovered in Europe in the late 1700s, a "golden age of porcelain" was launched. Artisans of Meissen, Limoges, and Royal Copenhagen, to name a few, created pieces of surpassing elegance that are cherished by collectors today.

embroidered napkin, for that matter). Another has not only become an expert on blue-and-white English transferware from 1790 to 1830, but has styled her dining room ∼ from wallpaper to

We always had our tea out of those blue cups when I was a little girl, sometimes in the queerest lodgings, and sometimes on a trunk in the theater.
∼ Willa Cather, *Alexander's Bridge*

needlepoint chair seats ∼ to complement her collection. Since teacups (especially the handles) are perilously fragile, some we discover are orphans, perhaps survivors of a fine set of Meissen or Sèvres made long ago. Let fancy be your guide, then, and pick only the prettiest for a mixed collection in which each cup is a dazzling individual.

And if one day you find yourself in yet another cluttered little shop, turning over a saucer to study the maker's mark, running a finger around the rim to check for nicks, holding a cup to the light to detect repairs, you'll know it for sure: You've become a collector.

Wedgwood

And if it is also stamped "Wedgwood," you hold in your hands a work of one of England's longest-thriving pottery firms, whose wares have been prized since the 1770s. Its founder, the amazingly inventive Josiah Wedgwood I, worked years to perfect Jasper, right, adorned with delicate, cameo-like figures from classical mythology, and still the most recognizable of Wedgwood's many creations. His lovely creamware (called "Queen's ware" after Queen Charlotte acquired a tea set in 1765) graced

tables throughout Europe and America. Today, brides can pick from elegant patterns, new and historic, each piece proudly stamped "Wedgwood."

The miniature set above was created by Thomas Minton for Queen Mary's dollhouse, and bears her royal monogram. Other tiny tea things that collectors now love were originally made so traveling salesmen could tempt buyers with new patterns. The canteen case opposite, with its beautifully engraved silver teapot, dates to 1850 and belonged to an English officer in the Indian Army. It includes the "necessities" of life ⁓ items to brew and take tea, as well as a telescopic toasting fork.

A Collector's Cup

Clockwise from top left: four teacups from Limoge, "A la Reine" at front; "Lotus" teacup from Mikasa; "Blue Fluted" teacup from Royal Copenhagen; "Lady Carlyle" teacup from Royal Doulton; "Samoa" teacup from Jean Louis Coquet.

Clockwise from top right: "Blue Willow" teapot from Spode; "Hawthorn" teapot from Emma Bridgewater; polka-dot stacking teapot and cup from Shellie Kirkendall; 19th-century English antique; teapot inspired by a Colonial Williamsburg design.

A Collector's Pot

BEAUTIFULLY BREWED

Tea loves oxygen-rich water, so fill the kettle with cold water only.

Slosh boiling water in and out of the pot to warm it. Return the kettle to a full boil and pour the water over loose tea ⁓ about one teaspoon of tea per cup, unless you like it stronger. Add up to a tablespoon per cup for more delicate green teas.

Wide-based, round pots give the tea leaves space to unfurl.

How long to steep tea leaves? Generally, three to five minutes, depending on your preference, but never more than five: They turn bitter. For herbal and fruit infusions, steep four to eight minutes.

Tea bags hold leaves cut for speed; often steeping for a minute or two suffices.

AS CROWDED WITH BLOSSOMS AS AN ENGLISH cottage garden, chintzware, in a myriad of bygone patterns, is sought avidly by those who fall under its innocent spell. Despite today's climbing

The Glory of Chintz

prices, this was once humble daily china, a blithe flower show that brightened ordinary English homes and was just as cheerful as the fabric it was derived from. Indeed, the story is told of chintzware's originator, Leonard Grimwade, founder of the Royal Winton potteries in Stoke-on-Trent, that he once stopped a lady in the street so he could copy the floral pattern of her pinafore. In the heyday of chintzware ∼ the 1920s to the 1960s ∼ many potteries were turning out patterns with fetching names like "Julia," "Sunshine," "Hazel," and "Summertime," each a favorite of collectors today.

∼ Very little chintzware was made after the 1960s, so a complete "Summertime" tea set with its own tray is a rare find. Many collectors simply mix and merrily unmatch.

Intriguing shapes such as the square "Julia" sugar bowl, above, and overall patterns like those in the "Summertime" set, opposite, are part of chintzware's appeal. Paper patterns (which grew brighter after the 1940s) were applied to the china by hand, "so you want to make sure there are no wrinkles," advises collector Sheryl Lowe, whose prizes appear here. "I walk into a room, and there the chintzware sits in a sunbeam, catching my eye," she says. "It feels like someone smiling at you."

TEA IS SUCH A PLEASANT PART OF OUR LIVES

that its accoutrements have a sly way of escaping the table to join the general decor. Indeed, the mere facts that we might have a round, pedestal

A Tea Lover's Home

tea table, anchoring a bouquet of tea roses (named for their evocatively similar scent), and that we set our table and measure our cooking ingredients with teaspoons, are proof positive that tea has long been at home with us. But why stop there? Enlisting a favorite teapot or creamer to hold a clutch of wildflowers is only a beginning. One collector found herself selecting fabrics and rugs that played happily into the mood of her tea sets. Another tea lover ornaments her dining room sideboard with a handsome Russian samovar; still another hangs her grandmother's perforated silver tea balls (once used to steep loose

Creating a space to enjoy your morning cup is one joy of collecting. A decorating scheme that blends casual comfort with evocations of the past lends itself well to a display of tea things, as cheerful to look at as they are to use. A cup given by a friend or a row of ceramic pots gathered on one's travels speak always of hospitality.

tea in a cup) on the Christmas tree ～ as gleaming family ornaments.

One particularly useful invention, the table whose tray top is detachable, makes it easy to carry tea things (or cocktails or canapés) in from

He brewed his tea in a blue china pot, poured it into a chipped white cup with forget-me-nots on the handles, and dropped in a dollop of honey and cream. 'I am,' he sighed deeply, 'contented as a clam.'

～ Ethel Pochocki, Wildflower Tea

the kitchen without having to clear a surface to set them on. When not a tray, it's a table; perfect for a smaller house. The kitchen is tea's cheerful home ground, a good place for a bit of whimsy in the wallpaper or a show of colorful crockery. If the tea blends you collect start to overflow their cabinet, why not dedicate an open shelf to them, all kept fresh in rows of the old-fashioned labeled tins with tight lids called caddies. Then whatever your mood, you'll quickly be able to reach for the right tea.

The Accoutrements of Tea

Tea for the Victorians was a chance to enjoy light conversation, heavy silver, and an impressive array of utensils.

Many finely crafted tea accessories were once absolute necessities. Through a strainer, right, tea steeped in the pot was cleansed of stray leaves as one poured; the spout could then be muffled to keep heat in, or the entire pot encased in a tea cozy, below. There were caddy spoons shaped like shells to measure the loose tea, tongs for the lumps of sugar, forks for the lemon slices, trivets set over a burner to keep the water pot hot. Today we regard such items as perforated silver muffin dishes (steam from

below kept them warm) as elegant curios for collectors ∽ but think how gratifying it was to be offered warmth along with beauty in a chilly parlor!

Linen tea towels (these above printed with a bold reminder that they are not to be called "dish towels") keep marching off their rack. It's possible to have your cup and delightful café curtains, too. A lighthearted decorating touch, opposite, brings teacups to printed upholstery cottons and pillow shams. If blue-and-white Staffordshire is your cup of tea, why not flaunt your passion on a wallpaper border, stencil, needlepoint pillow ⁓ even stationery ⁓ as well?

IN ONE CORNER, A WEARY SHOPPER SETS down her bags; nearby a couple chats intently, lingering over their cups and cakes. Across the room, a young girl and her mother burst into

Visit a Tearoom

giggles when both reach simultaneously for a tiny lemon tart. There's the happy clink of spoons and the smell of good baking in the air. Tearooms, even in strange towns, have a neighborly air, as if they'd been expecting you all along. The decor needn't be fancy: Some of England's most popular tearooms are simple and homey. In America, in recent years, tearooms that serve up old-fashioned charm along with sumptuous pastries have been opening faster than roses in June, some with a list of gourmet teas as long as a four-star wine list. A few are almost clubs, uniting tea lovers through special

Plain or fancy, the recipe for a successful tearoom always includes a mysterious "aaahhh" ~ that time-honored blend of kindly attention, steaming pots hustled to the table, and the certainty of something utterly indulgent on the fork.

When your feet tell you you've seen enough exhibits for today, or you gave up lunch for art, nothing is more welcome than settling down with a teatime menu at a historic house or museum.

events topped off with strawberries and whipped cream. And if the scones or the tea cakes have gained a faithful following, you may even find a bakery attached to your favorite tearoom with delicacies to take home.

The classic little tearoom on the village high street is not the only place to seek the solace of a cup and delicate tea sandwich. Some of the most delightful venues are in museums and historic houses, and partake of their unique atmospheres; many offer special-event teas as well. Travelers, too, are delighted to discover how many full-service inns and even bed-and-breakfasts have embraced this cosseting custom, knowing that a relaxing atmosphere ⁓ a cozy Victorian parlor, a verandah with wicker chairs, or a garden patio where a fountain plays ⁓ is often as important to those far from home as the sustenance itself. If so, they've learned the secrets of the tearoom, a place of reliable warmth and welcome.

A Tea Salon Owner

Make a reservation at Jennifer Johnson's Chez Nous in Seattle, and you are welcomed into her home, where a fire glows in the foyer, the colorful tablecloths are set with her own white Italian china, and a complete English tea is served at 2:30 PM. As Jennifer tempts you with hot buttered cheese scones ⁓ a mere appetizer for what follows ⁓ a concert pianist segues from show tunes to Chopin, and everyone settles back for a delicious afternoon.

It's very much the sort of teatime Jennifer knew growing up in London, where her mother would give parties for her friends. "But more indulgent," she admits, "because I serve three savories and three sweets, followed by a classic trifle in a champagne glass ⁓ my Auntie's recipe. I advise people not to have lunch before-

hand!" What's amazing is that Jennifer does all the baking, serving, and even the laundering herself, except when she enlists her husband, Chuck, when the crowd grows to over eighteen people. "Not everyone is crazy enough to open their own residence to the public," she laughs. But since her dining room and two flanking living rooms are commercially zoned, and she has been a professional chef, she took a chance that coffee-mad Seattle would love a true English afternoon tea, right down to the house-blend Earl Grey and egg salad sandwiches. "Word of mouth has been our best advertisement," she says. "Now most of the people who come ⁓ students, couples, people celebrating a birthday ⁓ come back. They seem to love the relaxation and cheerful, homey atmosphere."

Sweet Onion Tart

To evoke a gentle tea salon mood, even your savory dishes should have a light and airy touch. Here, sweet onions such as Vidalia or Walla Walla "lift" the flavor of this otherwise hearty tart. Lapsang souchong makes a good tea pairing with such savory delights.

PASTRY SHELL
1 cup all-purpose flour
Pinch of salt
½ cup (1 stick) cold unsalted butter, cut into bits
3 tablespoons ice water

SWEET ONION FILLING
6½ tablespoons unsalted butter
3 (8-ounce) sweet onions, thinly sliced
1 garlic clove, chopped
½ teaspoon chopped fresh thyme
Salt and freshly ground black pepper, to taste
½ cup dry white wine
5 tablespoons all-purpose flour
2 cups milk
Pinch of ground nutmeg
4 large eggs

Snipped fresh chives, for garnish

TO MAKE THE PASTRY SHELL

1. In a food processor, combine the flour and salt. Add the butter and pulse several times, until the mixture forms coarse crumbs.

2. With the processor running, gradually pour in the ice water, processing until the dough forms a ball. Shape the dough into a disk. Wrap the dough in plastic wrap and refrigerate for at least 1 hour.

TO MAKE THE SWEET ONION FILLING

3. In a large nonstick skillet over medium-low heat, melt 1½ tablespoons butter. Add the onions, garlic, thyme, and salt and pepper. Stir in the wine and cook, stirring often, for 20 to 30 minutes, until the onions are golden brown and soft. Remove the skillet from the heat and let the mixture cool.

4. Preheat the oven to 375°F.

5. In a medium-size saucepan over medium heat, melt the remaining 5 tablespoons butter. Whisk in the flour and cook, stirring constantly, for 2 to 3 minutes. Gradually whisk in the milk and cook, whisking constantly, until the mixture boils. Remove the saucepan from the heat and season with nutmeg and salt and pepper. Transfer the mixture to a large bowl.

6. Break the eggs into a medium-size bowl and beat. Whisk three large spoonfuls of the hot milk mixture into the eggs until blended. Whisk the egg mixture back into the milk mixture in the bowl. Add the onions and mix until well combined.

7. On a lightly floured surface, roll out the dough to an 11-inch round. Fit it into a 9-inch pie plate. Pour the onion filling into the pastry shell, spreading it evenly.

8. Bake for 25 to 30 minutes, until the custard is just set. Let the tart cool for 10 minutes on a wire rack.

9. Serve garnished with snipped chives.

Makes: 6 servings

Nasturtium Sandwiches

Aside from their delightfully peppery taste, the great virtue of these tiny tea sandwiches is their simplicity. Cut the bread as thin as you can for the most delicate offering. Day-old bread is easiest to cut, but if you must work with fresh bread, use a hot knife to slice it.

> 1 (4-ounce) package softened cream cheese
>
> 8 thin slices brown bread with crusts removed, or slices of focaccia
>
> Unsalted butter, softened, for spreading
>
> 1½ cups pesticide-free nasturtium flowers and leaves

1. In the medium-size bowl of an electric mixer, at high speed, beat the cream cheese until light and fluffy. Set aside.
2. Thinly spread each slice of bread with butter. Top half the buttered slices with the cream cheese, spreading it evenly. Arrange the flowers over the cream cheese, making sure to extend some of the petals over the edges of the bread. Cover with the remaining bread and press it into place. Cut each sandwich into 2 fingers.
3. Serve, or cover with plastic wrap and refrigerate for up to 4 hours.

Makes: 8 sandwiches

Lavender Tea

Imagine sitting down in a London tea salon after a long afternoon of shopping. The "nippy," the old-fashioned term for a tea server, brings you a restorative pot exuding the heady scent of lavender, a natural energizer. Minutes later, you feel refreshed and ready to take on Savile Row.

> 3 fresh pesticide-free lavender flowers or ⅓ teaspoon dried
>
> 4 teaspoons orange pekoe tea
>
> Lavender honey, to taste

1. Pour boiling water into the teapot and set aside for 5 minutes. Discard the water.
2. Gently crush the lavender leaves to release their flavor, put them into into a tea ball, and add the tea. Cover the tea ball and place in the teapot. Cover with about 6 cups boiling water and let steep for 5 minutes. Remove the tea ball and serve the tea with lavender honey on the side.

Makes: 4 to 6 servings

Walnut-Pepper Biscotti

According to the Chinese ∼ the original tea connoisseurs ∼ there are just five flavors: bitter, salty, sour, hot, or sweet. This recipe definitely falls into more than one category, as the heat of the pepper balances the subtle sweetness of the walnuts. For a more intense flavor, use black walnuts.

> 1¾ cups all-purpose flour
> ½ teaspoon baking soda
> ½ teaspoon baking powder
> ⅛ teaspoon salt
> 1½ teaspoons freshly ground black
>   pepper
> ½ cup (1 stick) unsalted butter, softened
> 1 cup sugar
> 2 large eggs, at room temperature
> 2 teaspoons grated orange zest
> 1½ teaspoons vanilla extract
> ¼ teaspoon almond extract
> 1½ cups walnuts, lightly toasted and
>   chopped

1. Sift the flour, baking soda, baking powder, and salt into a large bowl. Add the pepper.

2. In the large bowl of an electric mixer, at medium speed, cream the butter. Add the sugar a little at a time, then beat the mixture until light and fluffy. Beat in the eggs one at a time, then beat in the orange zest, vanilla, and almond extract. Beat in the flour mixture until just combined, then stir in the walnuts. Shape the dough into a ball and wrap in plastic wrap. Chill for several hours, or overnight.

3. Preheat the oven to 350°F. Butter and flour two baking sheets.

4. Divide the dough into three pieces. With lightly floured hands, roll each piece into a log 1½ inches in diameter. Transfer two logs to one baking sheet, spacing them 5 inches apart. Place the third log on the second baking sheet. Bake for 20 minutes, or until golden. Let cool slightly on the sheets, then cut the logs crosswise into ¾-inch-thick diagonal slices. Turn the slices cut side down on the baking sheets and bake about 15 minutes, or until golden brown. Transfer the biscotti to wire racks and let cool completely. Store in an airtight container.

Makes: about 3 dozen biscotti

Lavender Sorbet

A cup of warm Lavender Tea perfectly complements this frosty, palate-cleansing dessert.

> 2½ cups water
> ½ cup sugar
> 4 heads pesticide-free lavender flowers
> Juice of 1 lemon
> Pesticide-free lavender flowers,
>   for garnish

1. In a medium-size saucepan over medium heat, combine 1 cup water and the sugar. Bring the mixture to a simmer, stirring, and cook the syrup until it is clear. Remove from the heat and let cool completely.

2. In a large saucepan, combine 1 cup of the syrup with the lavender flowers and half the lemon juice. Slowly bring the mixture to a boil over medium-high heat, stirring constantly. Remove from the heat, cover, and let cool completely.

3. Strain the syrup through a fine-mesh sieve into a bowl. Add the remaining 1½ cups water. Add the remaining lemon juice if the mixture seems too sweet.

4. Transfer the mixture to an ice-cream machine and freeze according to the manufacturer's instructions.

5. Let the sorbet stand in the refrigerator for 10 minutes before serving. Spoon into decorative ice cream dishes or stemmed glasses. Garnish with the fresh lavender flowers and serve immediately.

Makes: about 1½ pints

Canadian Chocolate Cake

Canadians have long been avid tea drinkers — tea made up a substantial part of the cargoes delivered to the early settlers from England. To accompany their favorite beverage, pioneer families also savored baked goods whose fresh taste could be ensured over long journeys, such as this chocolate cake made with zucchini for moistness.

1⅓ cups sugar
3 large eggs
3 cups grated zucchini
½ cup chopped walnuts
7 ounces grapeseed oil (available at specialty-food markets), or vegetable oil
7 ounces bittersweet chocolate, melted
1½ cups self-rising cake flour, sifted

1. Preheat the oven to 325°F. Butter a 9-inch cake pan, line it with parchment or waxed paper, and butter the paper. Set aside.

2. In a large bowl, beat the sugar and eggs until well combined. Stir in the zucchini, walnuts, oil, and chocolate. Add the flour a little at a time and blend until combined.

3. Transfer the batter to the prepared pan, smoothing it into an even layer. Bake for 1¼ hours, or until a toothpick inserted in the center comes out clean.

4. Let the cake cool in the pan on a wire rack for 5 minutes, then invert onto the rack and let cool completely.

Makes: 6 to 8 servings

Celebrations

Bring out the best cups and dessert plates ∽ company is coming for tea! The appeal of a tea party has particular resonance in our hurried modern lives: A sweet indulgence held at a civilized hour, a way to fête all ages, a relaxing respite from the everyday ∽ a tea party honors your guests with a graceful touch of ceremony.

THEY MAY BOUNCE ON THEIR BEDS AND HANG

by their knees from trees, but sooner or later, all

little girls like pretending to be grown-up ladies. It's

a wish worth indulging with a children's tea party,

For the Children

for along with yummy things to eat comes a lesson

in good-host graces, from picking and arranging

the daisies to making the lemonade and deciding

who sits where (and why). And besides, it's fun.

One birthday idea is a dress-up tea party, at

which both boys and girls can rummage through

old-fashioned garb (including loopy beads and

outrageous bow ties) gleaned from thrift shops to

assemble their own costumes. For girls, hat deco-

rating is a great party game. All it requires are some

plain hats and lots of ribbon, scarves or snippets,

silk flowers, and glue; each girl dons her glamorous

creation for teatime and then wears it home.

For a summertime tea in the garden, young hostesses invent with what's on hand: mint in abundance for the iced tea, a watering pot for a fresh-plucked bouquet. No need to be formal here, where butterflies arrive uninvited.

Grandparents always know how to make something special. To help their visiting grandchildren find playmates, this couple has invited some neighbor children to a party the youngsters helped plan. With one morning spent picking strawberries, another making cookies, and much discussion about where to set the table ～ what if it rains? ～ the days of preparation flew by. Even before the guests arrived, the grandkids felt they had some wonderful best friends: Grandma and Grandpa.

**And is there honey
still for tea?**

⁓ Rupert Brooke,
"The Old Vicarage, Grantchester"

Honey Tea Sandwiches

Straight from the heart of the Cotswolds, this recipe involves baking your own honey quick bread and cutting it into decorative shapes. Try making these with different kinds of tea, such as chamomile or apple mint. The simple sandwich filling is a silky mix of lemon and banana.

¾ cup hot strong brewed tea
¾ cup packed brown sugar
⅓ cup honey
2 cups unbleached all-purpose flour
1½ teaspoons baking soda
1 banana
1 teaspoon fresh lemon juice
Chocolate drop candies or colored
    sprinkles, for garnish

1. Preheat the oven to 350°F. Butter and flour an 8½- by 4½- by 2½-inch loaf pan.

2. Divide the tea between two small bowls. Stir the brown sugar into one bowl until dissolved. Stir the honey into the other bowl until dissolved. Set both bowls aside.

3. In a medium-size bowl, combine the flour and baking soda. Stir in the sugar-tea mixture until blended. Quickly stir in the honey-tea mixture until blended. Pour the batter into the prepared pan.

4. Bake for 40 to 45 minutes, until a toothpick inserted in the center comes out clean. Cool the bread in the pan on a wire rack for 10 minutes. Remove from the pan and cool the bread on the wire rack.

5. In a medium-size bowl, mash the banana with the lemon juice.

6. Trim off the ends of the bread. Cut the loaf into ½-inch-thick slices. With a 1¾- to 2-inch cookie cutter, cut a flower shape from each slice. With a sharp paring knife or a very small round cookie cutter, cut a ½-inch hole in the center of half the flowers.

7. Spread the solid bread flowers with the banana mixture. Top with the remaining slices. Fill the holes with the chocolate drops. Serve at once.

Makes: 6 or 7 sandwiches

Vanilla Milk Tea

Here is just the sort of velvety-sweet tea served in an English nursery at midday to help sustain children through energetic afternoons. This recipe calls for English breakfast, a blend of black teas from Ceylon and India, which is tailor-made to go with milk (as are all black teas).

1 cup milk
One 2-inch piece vanilla bean, split
4 teaspoons English breakfast tea

1. Pour the milk into a small saucepan. Add the split vanilla bean and bring to a simmer, stirring often. Remove the saucepan from the heat and let stand until the milk is cool. Remove the vanilla bean.

2. Brew the tea according to the package directions. Pour the tea into warmed mugs and top with the vanilla milk.

Makes: 4 to 5 servings.

Lemon Cupcakes

Dressed up with sprigs of herbs, these elegant cupcakes can be served to children and adults with equal success.

½ cup milk
¼ cup chopped fresh lemon balm, lemon thyme, or lemon verbena
2 teaspoons grated lemon zest
3 tablespoons fresh lemon juice
2 cups sifted all-purpose flour
½ teaspoon baking soda
¼ teaspoon salt
½ cup (1 stick) softened unsalted butter
1¼ cups granulated sugar
2 large egg yolks, at room temperature
3 large egg whites, at room temperature, stiffly beaten
2 cups confectioners' sugar
2 tablespoons heavy cream
Lemon balm, lemon thyme, or lemon verbena sprigs, for garnish (optional)

1. Preheat the oven to 350°F. Butter and flour twenty-one 2½-inch muffin cups or line them with paper muffin cups.

2. In a small saucepan, combine the milk and lemon balm. Bring to just under a simmer over medium heat. Remove the saucepan from the heat and let steep until the milk has cooled. Strain the milk through a fine-meshed sieve into a small bowl; discard the solids. Stir the lemon zest and 1 tablespoon lemon juice into the milk (the mixture will curdle); set aside.

3. In a medium-size bowl, stir together the flour, baking soda, and salt.

4. In the small bowl of an electric mixer, at medium speed, cream the butter. Gradually add the granulated sugar, beating until the mixture is light and fluffy. Add the egg yolks one at a time, beating well after each addition. Add the flour mixture alternately with the milk mixture, beating until smooth after each addition. Gently fold in the egg whites. Spoon the batter into the muffin cups, filling them halfway.

5. Bake for 15 to 18 minutes, until a toothpick inserted in the center comes out clean. Remove the cupcakes from the pans and cool completely on wire racks.

6. Sift the confectioners' sugar into the medium-size bowl of an electric mixer. With the mixer at medium speed, gradually add the cream and the remaining 2 tablespoons lemon juice. Beat the icing until it is smooth and spreadable.

7. Frost the cooled cupcakes with the icing. Transfer to a platter and garnish the cupcakes with fresh herbs, if desired.

Makes: 21 cupcakes

**EXCUSES TO HAVE
A TEA PARTY**

Your mother or sister
has come to visit: Invite your
friends to meet her.

A play (or concert or benefit
drive) is a huge success:
Have the whole gang over for
thanks, reunion ~ and tea.

Long-time friends are leaving
the neighborhood: Let them
know how much they'll be
missed at a tea to which everyone contributes a confection.

Your best friend is
expecting a child: Host a
shower in her honor.

You want to start a book
group: Invite everyone
interested to meet each other
and work out the game plan.

The garden has never been
lovelier: Put chairs and tables
outside and share the splendid
results of your labors.

Hold a gourmet tea-tasting:
Let each guest bring
her favorite tea (and her
own pot) and tell the others
all about her choice.

TEA IS LIKE A HUG AND A HANDSHAKE;

something about it warms friendships and

inspires confidences. Though we don't always

stand on ceremony with good friends ⁓ mugs will

Among Friends

do for that marathon chat at the kitchen table ⁓

it's also fun to honor them with the flourish of a

tea nicely presented. Whether you invite four or

fourteen to tea, stick to what works best for your

own home and personal style. Though in an

earlier day the hostess poured, asking each guest

in turn his or her preference, you might let them

fix their own tea (made ahead very strong) and

dilute it with hot water to taste. Small tables

within reach ⁓ no one really likes balancing a

cup and saucer on a knee ⁓ and miniature, var-

ied delectables that fingers or little plates can

handle gracefully help put everyone at ease.

⁓ *Remember your childhood view of a tea party ⁓ pinkies raised, everyone stiff and formal? Yet a grown-up tea can be the most relaxed of gatherings, a time for laughter and sharing. The point of a party among good friends is the company itself, and the pleasure of feeling everyone's spirits rising with the tea steam.*

Celebrate the strawberry season and a warm day with a picnic tea party. Pack a thermos of tea, iced or hot, fresh berries and scones, dishes muffled in cloth napkins, and venture out of doors. You don't have to hike up a mountain to appreciate the manna that tea ∽ thirst-quenching, restorative, and sweetened as you like ∽ is to the wanderer.

English Scones

The remarkable thing about scones is that on their own they are the simplest of plain risen cakes. But lavish on the jam and clotted cream (or lashings of butter), and they become quite sumptuous indeed. For best results, bake these just before your party.

> 1⅔ cups self-rising cake flour
> ½ teaspoon baking powder
> 2 tablespoons sugar
> ½ teaspoon salt
> ¼ cup (½ stick) cold unsalted butter, cut into bits
> 1 large egg
> ½ cup plus 2 tablespoons milk, plus additional for glazing
> Fresh jam and clotted cream, for serving

1. Preheat the oven to 425°F. Butter a baking sheet.

2. Sift the flour, baking powder, sugar, and salt together into a medium-size bowl. With a pastry blender or two knives, cut in the butter until the mixture resembles a coarse meal.

3. In a small bowl, beat together the egg and milk. Add the milk mixture a little at a time to the dry ingredients, stirring until a sticky dough forms.

4. Turn the dough out onto a lightly floured surface and roll it into a ¾-inch-thick round. Cut out the scones with a floured 2-inch cookie cutter. Arrange the scones about 1 inch apart on the prepared baking sheet and brush the tops with milk.

5. Bake the scones for 12 to 15 minutes, until the tops are lightly golden and the bottoms sound hollow when tapped.

6. Serve the scones on a platter with the jam and clotted cream on the side.

Makes: about 8 scones

Blackberry Iced Tea

The rich, deep flavors of orange pekoe and Darjeeling teas both lend themselves to the tartness of blackberries, but don't restrict yourself to this union. Try different kinds of fruit-and-tea combinations; for instance, sliced fresh peaches with amber-colored Formosa Oolong, whose taste has been likened to that of ripe peaches.

> ½ to 1 ounce pesticide-free marigold flowers
> 4 cups hot black tea, such as orange pekoe or Darjeeling
> 1 cup blackberries
> Honey, to taste

1. Remove the petals from the flowers.

2. Place 3 to 4 petals in each compartment of an ice-cube tray. Fill the compartments halfway with water and freeze for at least 2 hours. Fill each compartment to the top with water and freeze until solid.

3. In a medium-size bowl, combine the hot tea with the blackberries. Set aside to steep for 1 hour.

4. With the back of a wooden spoon, crush the berries against the side of the bowl. Pour the mixture through a fine-meshed sieve into a pitcher, pressing on the solids

with the back of the spoon to extract all the liquid; discard the solids. Add honey to taste and chill for at least 2 hours.

5. Serve in tall glasses with the marigold ice cubes.

Makes: about 4 servings

Goat Cheese Toasts with Pink Peppercorns

Amuse-bouches, *or bite-size canapés, both tempt the appetite and enhance a buffet display. Choose a young mild goat cheese, such as Montrachet or Chavrous.*

> ½ loaf French bread (baguette), cut into ¼-inch-thick slices
> 1 (11-ounce) log goat cheese, cut into ¼-inch-thick slices
> 2 tablespoons extra-virgin olive oil
> Pink peppercorns
> Leaves from ½ bunch fresh thyme

1. Preheat the broiler. Arrange the bread slices on an ungreased baking sheet. Broil the bread 3 to 4 inches from the heat for 1 to 2 minutes, until toasted.

2. Turn the slices over, top with the goat cheese, drizzle lightly with the oil, and sprinkle each toast with a few peppercorns and thyme leaves. Broil for 1½ to 2 minutes, until the cheese is warm and the edges of the bread are toasted.

Makes: 16 to 20 toasts

Cucumber-Basil Tea Sandwiches

Basil complements the sweetness of English cucumber, making these traditional tea sandwiches something special. To make them even fancier, "frill" the cucumber with a fork drawn lengthwise down it before slicing.

> 1 (8-ounce) package softened cream cheese
> 2 tablespoons half-and-half
> 2 tablespoons snipped fresh chives
> 1 unsliced loaf or 12 slices rye or whole-wheat bread
> 1 English (seedless) cucumber, cut into thin slices
> 24 fresh basil leaves

1. In a medium-size bowl, beat together the cream cheese and half-and-half until it is the consistency of soft butter. Stir in the chives.

2. If you are using an unsliced loaf of bread, slice 12 thin slices from it. With a 2½-inch round cookie cutter, stamp out two rounds from each slice of bread. Spread the cheese mixture on the bread rounds, then top each with several slices of cucumber and a basil leaf. Serve the sandwiches immediately, or cover with plastic wrap and refrigerate until ready to serve.

Makes: 24 sandwiches

Ruby Tea Biscuits

Though these gleaming biscuits (ruby red from the jam or jelly) could crown the fanciest tables, they're also wonderful to serve at a last-minute informal lunch. They can be made in a pinch because most of the ingredients are already in your kitchen, and you can top them with any kind of red preserves you like (cranberry, raspberry, and red currant are all delicious possibilities).

> 2 cups sifted all-purpose flour
> 2 tablespoons sugar
> 4 teaspoons baking powder
> $\frac{1}{2}$ teaspoon salt
> $\frac{1}{2}$ cup vegetable shortening
> $\frac{3}{4}$ cup milk
> 2 tablespoons red jam or jelly

1. Place an oven rack in the center of the oven. Preheat the oven to 425°F.

2. In a large mixing bowl, combine the flour, sugar, baking powder, and salt. Mix well with a fork. With a pastry blender or two knives, cut in the shortening until the mixture resembles a coarse meal. Add the milk and mix with a fork just until the dough forms a soft ball.

3. Turn the dough out onto a floured surface and lightly knead 12 times with floured hands. Flour a rolling pin and roll out the dough $\frac{1}{4}$ inch thick. With a floured 2-inch round cookie cutter, cut out the biscuits.

4. Using a spatula, lift half the circles, one at a time, onto an ungreased baking sheet, arranging them about 1 inch apart.

5. With a floured 1-inch round cutter, cut a hole in the center of the remaining biscuits to make rings. Lift out the dough centers with the spatula and set aside. With the spatula, place the rings on top of the dough circles on the cookie sheet.

6. Carefully fill the middle of each ring with $\frac{1}{2}$ teaspoon jam.

7. Bake for 12 to 15 minutes, until the biscuits are puffed and lightly golden. Transfer the biscuits to wire racks to cool slightly. If desired, bake the 1-inch centers for 10 to 12 minutes, until lightly golden.

8. Serve the biscuits on warm plates.

Makes: 12 biscuits (and centers)

Butter Sponge Cake

A variation on the rich Victorian sponge cake, this lighter version omits the buttercream and cuts the cake in half: Rather than two separate baked layers, it is made of one layer sliced into two extra-delicate tiers. Try serving Badamtam, a grand Darjeeling and wonderful tea-party beverage, with this.

¾ cup (1½ sticks) softened unsalted butter
¾ cup granulated sugar
3 large eggs
1½ cups all-purpose flour
1 teaspoon vanilla extract
1½ teaspoons baking powder
Raspberry jam, to taste
Confectioners' sugar, for garnish

1. Preheat the oven to 350°F. Butter and flour an 8-inch round cake pan.

2. In the medium-size bowl of an electric mixer, at medium speed, cream the butter and granulated sugar until light and fluffy. Add the eggs one at a time, adding 1 tablespoon of flour with each egg, and beating after each addition until well combined. Stir in the vanilla.

3. Sift the remaining flour and the baking powder into a medium-size bowl. Stir the dry ingredients into the butter mixture until blended. Pour the batter into the prepared pan, spreading it evenly.

4. Bake for 45 to 50 minutes, until a toothpick inserted in the center comes out clean.

5. Let the cake cool in the pan on a wire rack for 5 minutes. Invert the cake onto the wire rack and let it cool completely.

6. Using a serrated knife, cut the cake horizontally into two layers. Spread the raspberry jam over the bottom layer, then top with the remaining layer. Place a doily over the cake and sift a dusting of confectioners' sugar over the top for garnish. Remove the doily and serve.

Makes: 6 to 8 servings

Bay Leaf Honey

The pungent, woodsy aroma and faint cinnamon taste of bay leaf make it a nice, slightly spicy addition to honey. Drizzle this in your tea or spread it over scones and biscuits.

2 cups light unflavored honey
1 large bay leaf

1. In a small saucepan over low heat, stir the honey until warmed through. Place the bay leaf in a sterilized jar and pour in the warmed honey.

2. Cover and let stand for at least 1 week before using.

Makes: 2 cups

All the world's teas come from two varieties of one plant, an evergreen shrub called camellia sinensis. Differences derive from the region where it is grown, and in how the leaves are picked, processed, and cut.

A short distance from historic Charleston,
South Carolina, lies verdant Wadmalaw
Island. Cross a few bridges, drive in past
long rows of flat-topped, waist-high tea
bushes, and you have arrived at the 127-
acre Charleston Tea Plantation, the only
such commercial enterprise in the nation,
whose bright, fresh-tasting tea is savored
throughout the tea-loving South and
beyond. Attempts to grow tea in this sub-
tropical Low Country began as early as
1799. But it took the combination of Bill
Hall (a third-generation tea-taster) and
Mack Fleming (a tea horticulturalist), along
with the unique tea harvesting machine
Mack invented to really make it work.

"We started with acclimated tea plants
rescued from a nearby abandoned planta-

tion," says Bill. Between May and October,
the barge-like tea harvester moves slowly
over the pesticide-free green hedges, clipping
newborn leaves on the top of each row every
fifteen days. Since rain and sun, cold and
heat make for different-tasting leaves, how
does a tea like American Classic Tea main-
tain its consistent flavor? Well, that's the art.
"I sort each picking into one of fifteen storage
bins," says Bill, "and blend them carefully to
get our flavor. It's about the freshest tea you
can buy." In the factory the leaves are dried,
rolled, and packaged, yielding the light,
refreshing classic, as well as bergamot- and
raspberry-flavored variations. "We do everything here ourselves," says Bill; "it's like a
family farm. The pleasure is succeeding in
something no one else can do."

A Tea Grower

shines even brighter than the stone in her engage-

ment ring. It's a time when she longs to share her

joy with all her friends. A tea for a bride-to-be is

To Honor Love

one of the happiest of all events ∼ a reunion

about union ∼ and deserves your best efforts.

Collaborate with the engaged couple's parents to

pilfer childhood pictures of both (scan hers onto

the invitations, display his around the room), and

plot some heartfelt mischief for a wedding

shower tea party, such as silly souvenirs (her

camp archery award, framed as a Cupid's gift for

him; his kindergarten report card for her). Invite

her oldest friend to dredge up memories of their

shared childhood; or, if you dare, ask the groom

twenty questions ahead of time ∼ and see if she

can guess his answers! Though you may not want

∼ *Neither a luncheon nor a dinner, an afternoon tea invites imagination to the table. When love is the theme, use flowers and herbs that bore symbolic messages in the past: rosemary for remembrance, roses for passion, violets for fidelity.*

When girlfriends gather to celebrate an upcoming wedding, it's impossible to be too romantic. Set the table, or a variety of small tables, with your finest china, or use those beautifully mismatched little plates, teacups, and saucers you've been collecting over the years, and indulge everyone with confections as artful as they are delicious.

to make the party itself a surprise, some guests can be ~ especially a dear friend from far away.

For this occasion, choose a romantically pastel color scheme for table linens, candles, placecards, and flowers, and don't be shy about asking to borrow a friend's pretty cake stand or silver teapot. A well-organized hostess gets others to contribute ~ and they'll want to. When guests arrive, it's thoughtful to have tea and plates of cookies or pastries ready to greet them, even if you intend to serve little sandwiches later ~ it warms up the party while you wait for latecomers, and gives the bride-to-be a chance to visit with everyone.

When it comes to gifts, why not make them themed to tea? Silver teaspoons, pretty cups, a needlepoint tea caddy, or some crochet-edged napkins ~ they'll remind her of this gathering always, and inspire her to invite you all back to tea when she's a married woman.

Watercress Sandwiches

If you have a few extra minutes before company arrives, make these sandwiches even fancier: dip the edges of the watercress sprigs used for garnish into paprika.

> 1 large bunch watercress
> 30 pesticide-free nasturtium flowers
> 1 (8-ounce) package softened cream cheese
> ½ cup peeled, seeded, and finely chopped cucumber
> 2 to 4 tablespoons very finely chopped yellow onion, to taste
> ¼ teaspoon salt
> ⅛ teaspoon freshly ground black pepper
> 8 slices fine-grained country white, wheat, or egg bread

1. Reserve 16 watercress sprigs for garnish. Chop enough of the remaining watercress leaves to make ½ cup. Reserve 8 nasturtium flowers for garnish. Cut the remaining nasturtium flowers into a fine julienne. Set both aside.

2. In a medium-size bowl, combine the cream cheese, cucumber, onion, chopped watercress, julienned nasturtium flowers, salt, and pepper. Mix well. Cover the mixture with plastic wrap and let stand for 1 hour to allow the flavors to blend.

3. Generously spread the cream cheese mixture onto the bread slices. Cut the sandwiches in half and transfer them to a serving plate. Garnish with the reserved watercress sprigs and nasturtium flowers.

Makes: 16 sandwiches

Smoked Salmon Canapés

Just as semisweet, delicate wines are traditionally served with smoked fish, these salmon appetizers are a wonderful foil for Strawberry Iced Tea, subtly lightened with lemon, sugar, and strawberries. If you can't get tobiko, substitute golden (whitefish) caviar instead.

> 6 slices dark rye cocktail bread
> 2 ounces thinly sliced smoked salmon
> 2 (3-ounce) packages cream cheese with chives, softened
> About 2 tablespoons tobiko (flying fish roe, available at Japanese markets), for garnish
> Dill sprigs, for garnish

1. Cut each slice of bread diagonally in half. Decoratively top each piece of bread with a thin strip of salmon.

2. Place the cream cheese in a pastry bag fitted with a number 1 tip. Pipe a rosette of cream cheese on top of each piece of salmon.

3. Transfer the sandwiches to serving plates and garnish each sandwich with a small spoonful of tobiko and a sprig of dill.

Makes: 12 sandwiches

To keep your teapot smelling fresh, store it with a sugar cube inside and the lid off.

Rose Petal Scones

Inspired by Middle Eastern cooking, these pretty, delicate scones, shown at top of the plate in the picture below, are flavored with rose water and pistachios.

2¼ cups all-purpose flour

2 teaspoons granulated sugar

2 teaspoons baking powder

½ teaspoon baking soda

¾ teaspoon salt

⅛ teaspoon ground cinnamon

¼ cup (½ stick) cold unsalted butter, cut into bits

⅓ cup shelled and peeled pistachios, lightly toasted and coarsely ground

1 cup heavy cream

1 teaspoon rose water

2 tablespoons thinly sliced pesticide-free rose petals

1 cup confectioners' sugar

1 tablespoon rose jelly, or 1 tablespoon red currant jelly mixed with ½ teaspoon rose water

2 to 3 teaspoons water

1. Preheat the oven to 425°F. Lightly butter a baking sheet.

2. Sift the flour, sugar, baking powder, baking soda, salt, and cinnamon together into a large bowl. With a pastry blender or two knives, cut in the butter until the mixture resembles a coarse meal. Stir in the pistachios.

3. In a small bowl, combine the cream, rose water, and rose petals. Add to the flour mixture and stir to form a soft dough.

4. Place the dough in heaping tablespoonfuls about 1 inch apart on the prepared baking sheet. Bake for 10 to 12 minutes, until the scones are golden brown. Transfer the scones to a wire rack set over a jelly-roll pan.

5. In a medium-size bowl, whisk together the confectioners' sugar, jelly, and water until smooth, adding additional water if needed. Drizzle the icing over the warm scones. Serve immediately.

Makes: about 24 scones

Heart Cookies

For a dotted swiss look that mimics bridal finery, pipe the icing out of small pastry bags, making tiny circlets.

2½ cups all-purpose flour
½ teaspoon salt
1 cup (2 sticks) unsalted butter, softened
⅔ cup granulated sugar
1 large egg
2 cups confectioners' sugar
About ¼ cup milk
Food coloring (optional)

1. In a medium-size bowl, stir together the flour and salt. Set aside.

2. In the large bowl of an electric mixer, at medium speed, cream the butter and granulated sugar until light and fluffy. Add the egg and mix until blended. Gradually beat in the flour mixture at low speed, just until blended.

3. Divide the dough in half. Form each half into a disk and wrap in plastic wrap. Refrigerate the dough for 2 hours.

4. Preheat the oven to 350°F.

5. On a lightly floured surface, roll out the dough ⅛ inch thick. With a 2½-inch heart-shaped cookie cutter, cut out as many hearts as possible. Arrange the hearts 1 inch apart on ungreased baking sheets.

6. Bake for 7 to 8 minutes, until the cookies start to brown.

7. Meanwhile, sift the confectioners' sugar into a medium-size bowl. Stir enough of the milk to form an icing with a runny consistency. Add the food coloring to tint the icing, if desired.

8. Spread the icing on the hot cookies. Cool the iced cookies on wire racks placed over waxed paper.

Makes: 48 cookies

Rose Petal Jam

Not entirely a jam but more like a pourable "honey" in consistency, this ambrosial topping for toast, muffins, or vanilla ice cream is best made with rose water, an intensely fragrant essence that must be used sparingly.

1½ cups lightly packed pesticide-free
    rose petals
1½ cups water
1⅓ cups sugar
¼ cup fresh lemon juice
1 teaspoon rose water (optional)

1. Spread the rose petals out on a paper towel–lined plate. Snip out the bitter white heels and any brown spots on the petals.

2. In a large heavy-bottomed saucepan, combine the rose petals and water. Stir in the sugar, lemon juice, and rose water, if desired. Bring to a full rolling boil over medium-high heat, stirring constantly.

3. Reduce the heat to medium and continue to cook, stirring often to prevent sticking, for 25 to 30 minutes, until the mixture thickens. When the mixture is done, a

spoonful of jam will hold its shape when placed on a cold plate.

4. Remove the jam from the heat and ladle into two sterilized 6-ounce jars. Cover the tops with melted paraffin and store in a cool, dark place for up to 2 weeks.

Makes: 1¼ cups

Strawberry Iced Tea

If you don't want to use tea bags, sprinkle the juice from 2 or 3 strawberries pressed through a fine-meshed sieve onto 3–4 teaspoons loose tea leaves, allow them to dry, and then brew them. The touch of lemon cuts through the strawberry-and-sugar sweetness.

> 2 cups water
> 2 strawberry tea bags
> ¼ cup sugar
> Juice of half a lemon
> Strawberries, for garnish

1. In a large saucepan, bring the water to a full boil. Add the tea bags and sugar. Remove the saucepan from the heat, cover, and let steep for 5 minutes.

2. Remove and discard the tea bags. Stir the lemon juice into the tea mixture and cool to room temperature.

3. Serve over crushed ice, garnished with strawberries.

Makes: 2 to 3 servings

Iced Darjeeling and Fruit Tea

Only teas grown on the gentle slopes of Darjeeling, India, bear this special title. Darjeeling complements a wide range of foods, while also being flavorful enough to drink alone.

> 2 quarts water
> 8 teaspoons Darjeeling tea
> 1 cup sugar
> 5 whole cloves
> Zest and juice of 1 lime
> Zest and juice of 1 orange
> Lime wedges, for garnish

1. In a medium-size saucepan, bring 1 quart water to a full boil. Add the tea, remove the saucepan from heat, cover, and let stand for 5 minutes. Strain the mixture through a fine-meshed sieve into a large bowl; discard the solids. Cover and refrigerate the tea for at least 2 hours, or overnight.

2. In another medium-size saucepan, bring the remaining 1 quart water to a full boil. Add the sugar, cloves, and orange and lime zests. Bring the mixture back to a boil and cook for 5 minutes. Remove the saucepan from the heat and stir in the orange and lime juices.

3. Strain the sugar mixture through a fine-meshed sieve into the tea mixture. Cool to room temperature.

4. Serve the tea over crushed ice, garnished with the lime wedges.

Makes: 6 to 8 servings

THERE'S NO BETTER TIME TO HAVE A PARTY
than when the house is spiced with pine boughs,
the silver gleams, and a ribboned wreath adorns
the door. Whether it's a tree-trimming party by

A Christmas Tea

the fire or an afternoon open house, a Christmas
tea is the perfect way to include entire families,
from toddlers to grandparents. It's good to have a
punch table for the little ones, with snatchable
sweets like Christmas cookies that won't bring dis-
aster to a velvet dress. As a surprise, you might sit
them down for a special holiday cake, or follow old
family customs such as baking coins into a steamed

When it's late on Christmas Eve, and yet more ribbons need tying, a tea break is in order, with just a few of those cookies left out for Santa. As carols play, sit back for a moment and sip ⁓ it may help you remember where you hid the presents you can't find.

pudding. A hot tea spiced with cinnamon and
orange adds a festive aroma to the gathering. And
with sherry and port on the sideboard, as well as
sweets and savories to last the lingering hours,
you'll have truly shared a merry time with all.

**SOME HOMEMADE GIFT
IDEAS FOR THE TEA
LOVERS ON YOUR LIST:**

Tie up a selection of excellent
loose teas in little muslin bags,
then wrap plaid silk around them.
Add polished flea-market spoons
or sugar tongs for gleam.

Personalize a glass jam jar,
honey pot, or plate with safe
paints. Try a monogram, a line
of her favorite poem, or just
"Good Morning, Jane."

Make a tea caddy unique with
decoupage. Any upright, airtight
tin will work well.

Create a gift basket with a
stacked cup and pot for one,
along with teatime treats, teas,
jams, a floral honey, or deco-
rated sugar cubes.

Bake big sugar cookies in the
shape of teapots, and decorate
each one differently.

Create a tea-themed Christmas
tree ornament by mounting your
needlepoint cup or pot on a stiff
backing with a loop.

Turn plain cotton or linen
napkins into personal treasures
with your own appliqué or
embroidery.

Sorrel, Leek, and Mushroom Tart

Slightly sour sorrel leaves are tempered by rich eggs, cheese, and cream in this savory French tart ⏤ a traditional dish for celebrations.

TART SHELL

- 1½ cups all-purpose flour
- ¾ teaspoon salt
- 6 tablespoons (¾ stick) cold unsalted butter, cut into bits
- 2 tablespoons solid white vegetable shortening
- 3 to 4 tablespoons ice water

SORREL, LEEK, AND MUSHROOM FILLING

- 3 tablespoons unsalted butter
- 1 large leek, white part only, finely chopped (1 cup)
- ¼ pound cremini or white button mushrooms, thinly sliced
- 1 teaspoon fresh thyme
- ½ teaspoon salt
- 4 ounces sorrel or spinach, stemmed and sliced into thin ribbons
- 3 large eggs
- 1 cup heavy cream
- ½ cup grated Gruyère or Comté cheese
- ⅛ teaspoon freshly ground black pepper

TO MAKE THE TART SHELL

1. In a medium-size bowl, combine the flour and salt. With a pastry blender or two knives, cut in the butter and shortening until the mixture resembles a coarse meal.

2. Gradually add the ice water, tossing with a fork until the dough just clings together. Flatten the dough into a disk and wrap in plastic wrap. Refrigerate for at least 30 minutes.

3. Preheat the oven to 425°F.

4. On a lightly floured surface, roll out the dough to a 13-inch circle. Fit it into a 9-inch tart pan. Trim to ½ inch above the edge of the pan and flute the edge. Place the tart pan on a baking sheet. Line the tart shell with a double thickness of aluminum foil and fill with dried beans.

5. Bake the shell for 10 minutes. Remove the aluminum foil and beans. Using a fork, prick any puffy areas, and bake for 4 to 5 minutes longer, until the edges start to brown. Cool on a wire rack. Reduce the oven temperature to 375°F.

TO MAKE THE SORREL, LEEK, AND MUSHROOM FILLING

6. In a large skillet over medium heat, melt the butter. Add the leek and sauté until tender. Add the mushrooms, thyme, and salt. Sauté until the liquid from the mushrooms has evaporated.

7. Add the sorrel, stirring quickly, just until wilted, about 1 minute. Remove from the heat and let cool.

8. In a medium-size bowl, whisk the eggs and cream until well combined. Stir in the cheese, pepper, and leek mixture.

9. Pour the filling into the cooled pastry shell, spreading it evenly. Place the tart on a baking sheet and bake for 35 to 40 minutes, until the filling is firm and golden brown.

10. Cool the tart on a wire rack for 20 to 30 minutes before serving.

Makes: 6 to 8 servings

Garlic-Herb Cheese

This flavorful spread is even more enticing when pressed through a pastry tube to create appealing designs on top of open-faced tea sandwiches or crackers. This cheese improves in flavor after a day and may be kept for 2 to 3 days, covered and chilled. Bring to room temperature before serving.

- 1 pound softened cream cheese
- 2 tablespoons half-and-half or milk
- 2 tablespoons minced fresh parsley
- 1 tablespoon minced fresh marjoram
- 1 tablespoon minced fresh savory
- 2 garlic cloves, finely minced
- Salt, to taste
- Cayenne pepper, to taste
- 1 teaspoon herb or white-wine vinegar (optional)

1. In a medium-size bowl, whisk together the cream cheese and half-and-half. Add the herbs, garlic, salt, cayenne, and vinegar, if desired, and whisk to combine. Cover with plastic wrap and chill for at least 2 hours.

Makes: about 2 cups

The handle on a teacup was an English invention, adapted from tankards used for hot toddies. Small ceramic teacups without handles have been favored in China for a millennium.

Corn Bread Triangles

A homespun (and easy) recipe for corn bread becomes special with the addition of fresh, fragrant herbs. If stone-ground cornmeal is available, the results will be more delicate.

- 1¼ cups all-purpose flour
- 1 cup yellow cornmeal (preferably stone-ground)
- 2 tablespoons sugar
- 2 teaspoons baking powder
- 1 teaspoon salt
- 1¼ cups milk
- 2 teaspoons water
- 1 large egg
- ¼ cup vegetable oil
- 2 teaspoons fine herbs, such as savory, marjoram, thyme, or parsley

1. Preheat the oven to 375°F. Butter a 15- by 10-inch jelly-roll pan.
2. In a medium-size bowl, combine the flour, cornmeal, sugar, baking powder, and salt. Mix until well blended. Make a well in the center and add the milk, water, egg, and oil. Mix quickly just until blended (do not overmix). Spread the batter into the prepared pan and sprinkle with the herbs.
3. Bake the corn bread for 12 to 13 minutes, just until golden brown.
4. Using a sharp knife, cut the corn bread on the diagonal into 1½-inch wide strips. Cut the strips into triangles. Serve immediately or wrap in plastic wrap and then aluminum foil and freeze.

Makes: 8 to 10 servings

Zucchini-Pistachio Bread

For a slightly spicy frosting on this tempting loaf, use brewed black or oolong (semifermented) tea instead of water.

ZUCCHINI-PISTACHIO BREAD
  1½ cups all-purpose flour
  1½ teaspoons baking soda
  ¼ teaspoon ground cinnamon
  ¾ cup sugar
  2 large eggs
  ½ cup vegetable oil
  1 teaspoon vanilla extract
  ½ teaspoon salt
  1½ cups grated zucchini, squeezed dry
  1½ cups shelled and peeled pistachios,
    lightly toasted

VANILLA-SCENTED FROSTING
  1 large egg white
  ¾ cup sugar
  2½ tablespoons cold water
  ⅛ teaspoon cream of tartar
  ¾ teaspoon light corn syrup
  ½ teaspoon vanilla extract

TO MAKE THE ZUCCHINI-PISTACHIO BREAD

1. Preheat the oven to 350°F. Generously butter a 9- by 5- by 3-inch loaf pan.

2. Sift together the flour, baking soda, and cinnamon into a bowl.

3. In another bowl, whisk together the sugar, eggs, oil, vanilla, and salt. Add to the dry ingredients and stir until combined. Fold in the zucchini and pistachios.

4. Transfer the batter to the prepared pan and bake for 50 to 60 minutes, until a cake tester inserted in the center comes out clean.

5. Let the bread cool in the pan on a wire rack for 10 minutes. Invert onto the wire rack and cool completely.

TO MAKE THE VANILLA-SCENTED FROSTING

6. In the top of a double boiler set over simmering water, combine the egg white, sugar, water, cream of tartar, and corn syrup. Using a hand mixer, beat the mixture for 7 minutes, or until it is thick and fluffy. Beat in the vanilla.

7. Frost the top of the cooled cake. Allow the frosting to set before serving.

Makes: 6 to 8 servings

Honey Flan

The fragrance of this silken flan wafting from the kitchen will fill the house with just the right festive air for a celebration.

HONEY FLAN
  1⅓ cups sweet white wine, such as
    Sauternes or late-harvest Riesling
  ⅔ cup light flavored honey, such as
    fragrant lavender
  1 strip lemon zest
  1 sprig pesticide-free lavender or
    1 teaspoon dried
  5 large eggs
  1 large egg yolk
  3 tablespoons sugar

HONEY-SCENTED WHIPPED CREAM
  1 cup heavy cream
  2 tablespoons light flavored honey,
    such as fragrant lavender

  Pesticide-free rose petals, for garnish

1. In a medium-size heavy-bottomed sauce-pan over medium-high heat, combine the wine, honey, lemon zest, and lavender. Bring the mixture to a simmer, stirring constantly. Remove from the heat and cool.

2. Preheat the oven to 350°F.

3. Strain the wine mixture into a medium-size bowl. In a large bowl, gently whisk the eggs and egg yolk together until blended. Gently whisk in the wine mixture.

4. Spread the sugar in the bottom of an 8- by 1½-inch round glass cake dish. Bake the sugar for 15 to 30 minutes, until it melts and turns a medium caramel color. Cool on a wire rack for 5 minutes. Reduce the oven temperature to 325°F.

5. Pour the egg mixture over the caramelized sugar. Bake for 30 to 35 minutes, until just set in the center when gently shaken.

6. Cool the flan on the wire rack to room temperature.

7. Run a small sharp knife around the side of the dish to loosen the flan. Quickly and carefully invert the flan onto a serving dish.

TO MAKE THE HONEY-SCENTED
WHIPPED CREAM

8. In the small bowl of an electric mixer, at high speed, beat the cream until soft peaks form. Add the honey and beat until combined.

9. Cut the flan into wedges and serve with a dollop of the whipped cream. Garnish with the rose petals.

Makes: 6 to 8 servings

Orange-Clove Tea

Mingling citrus, tea leaves, and spice in a single mellow drink, this warming holiday tea is the perfect backdrop for a menu that combines the zestiness of garlic, the tartness of sorrel, and the sweetness of honey. For variety's sake, try this recipe with another, lesser-known black tea, Keemun, whose bright red liquor lends itself to holiday celebrations. Lapsang souchong, a slightly smoky black tea, would be another fine choice for this menu, as it complements spicy foods and cheese. Use cinnamon sticks as stirrers.

½ **orange, sliced**
Whole cloves
6 cups hot brewed orange pekoe tea

1. Cut each orange slice in half (so each piece is a semicircle) and stud the skin side with several whole cloves. Pour the tea into 6 cups. Float a cloved orange slice in each cup when serving. For extra flavor, add two orange slices to the pot while the tea is brewing.

Makes: 6 servings

A tea's "liquor" is its color and fragrance as it blooms under the boiling water in the pot.

Resources

Select Sources for Teas and Other Goods

Aphrodisia
264 Bleecker Street
New York, NY 10014
(212) 989-6440
herbal teas

Betty & Taylors of Harrogate
Parliament Street
Harrogate HG1 2QU
England
teas

British Gourmet Chandlers
45 Wall Street
Madison, CT 06443
(800) 842-6674
teas, fine china, tearoom

Celestial Seasonings
4600 Sleepytime Drive
Boulder, CO 80301
(800) 525-0347
teas; mail order

The Collector's Teapot
62-68 Tenbroeck Avenue
Kingston, NY 12402
(800) 724-3306
teapots, tea accessories

Concord Teacakes
59 Commonwealth Avenue
Concord, MA 01742
(978) 369-0260
baked goods; mail order

Confectionally Yours, Inc.
62 Gleason
Hyannis, MA 02601
(508) 775-4768
baked goods; mail order

Country Cottage Gifts
40 Bloomfield Avenue
Windsor, CT 06095
(860) 688-1450
tea accessories

Crossings
(800) 209-6141; (978) 456-8116
French epicurean specialties, baked goods, preserves, candies; mail order

The Cultured Cup
5346 Belt Line Road
Dallas, TX 75240
(888) 847-8327
www.theculturedcup.com
teas, tea accessories, jams, cookies

Dabney Herbs
P.O. Box 22061
Louisville, KY 40252
(502) 893-5198
herbal teas, green teas

Dancing Deer Baking Company
77 Shirley Street
Boston, MA 02119
(888) 699-3337; (617) 469-2021
muffins, cakes, other baked goods; mail order

Eastern Shore Tea Company
P.O. Box 84
Church Hill, MD 21623
(800) 542-6064
teas, tea blends; mail order

Empire Tea Services
(800) 790-0246
www.guystea.com
tea, tea accessories, scone mixes, shortbread; mail order

Grace Tea Company, Ltd.
50 West 17th Street
New York, NY 10011
(212) 255-2935
loose-leaf teas; mail order

Harney & Sons
11 Brook Street
Salisbury, CT 06068
(800) 832-8463
teas, tea accessories, tea foods, as well as a tasting room; mail order and retail

Jean-Louis Coquet
(800) 993-2580
fine china

Shellie Kirkendall
5834 Troth Street
Mira Loma, CA 91752
(909) 685-4790
pottery

Lisa's Tea Treasures
1875 South Bascom Avenue
Suite 165
Campbell, CA 95008
(408) 371-7377
tea, tea accessories, tea truffles, tearoom

The Little Teapot
9401 Montpellier Drive
Laurel, MD 20708
(301) 498-8486
teas, porcelain, English china, British foods, tea accessories; serve tea in the Montpellier Mansion twice a month

Mikasa
(800) 833-4631
fine china

Peconic River Herb Farm
2749 River Road
Calverton, NY 11933
(516) 369-0058
herbal teas; mail order

An offering from the Eastern Shore Tea Co.

R.C. Bigelow
P.O. Box 580
Cheshire, CT 06410
(800) 841-8158
teas; mail order

Red Crane Teas
(888) 4473-3272
sk@redcranteas.com
teas, tea accessories; mail order

Royal Copenhagen
(800) 431-1992
fine china

Royal Doulton
(800) 682-4462
fine china

Royal Tea Company
5628 Main Street
Trumbull, CT 06611
(203) 452-1006
tea caterer

San Francisco Herb Company
250 14th Street
San Francisco, CA 94103
(800) 227-4530
www.sfherb.com
herbal teas; mail order

Simpson & Vail
3 Quarry Road
Brookfield, CT 06804
(800) 282-8327; (203) 775-0240
www.svtea.com
*teas, tea accessories,
gourmet foods*

Smiling Cat Tea Merchants
407 North 5th Avenue
Ann Arbor, MI 48104
(800) 440-8327
www.smilingcattea.com
teas, tea accessories; mail order

SpecialTeas
(888) 365-6983
www.specialteas.com
*loose-leaf teas, tea accessories;
mail order*

St. John's Herb Garden
7711 Hillmeade Road
Bowie, MD 20720
(301) 262-5302
herbal teas; mail order

The Tea Chest
321 South Main Street, #34
Sebastopol, CA 95492
(800) 928-4858
www.theteachest.com
*teas, teaware, hand-crafted
ceramics & glassware; mail order*

The Teacup
2207 Queen Anne Avenue North
Seattle, WA 98109
(206) 283-5931
*teas, tea accessories; mail order
and retail*

Tea for Two
424 Forest Avenue
Laguna Beach, CA 92651
(949) 494-7776
teas, tea accessories

The Tea Merchant
119 Newbury Street
Boston, MA 02116
(617) 247-4288
*teas, gourmet tea foods, honeys,
chocolates*

Tea-N-Crumpets
817 Fourth Street
San Rafael, CA 94901
(415) 457-2495
*crumpets, teas, tea accessories;
mail order and retail*

TeaRose Designs
25 Prospect Street
Needham, MA 02492
(781) 455-8778
*tea cozies, fabrics, ribbons;
mail order*

Todd & Holland Tea Merchants
7577 Lake Street
River Forest, IL 60305
(708) 488-1136
www.todd-holland.com
*loose-leaf teas, tea accessories, tea
foods; mail order and retail*

Two for the Pot
200 Clinton Street
Brooklyn, NY 11201
(718) 855-8173
loose-leaf teas, tea accessories

Upton Tea Imports
231 South Street
Hopkinton, MA 01748
(800) 234-8327
www.uptontea.com
*loose-leaf teas, accessories; mail
order and retail*

Victoria Collection
Dept. VC191
P.O. Box 400835
Des Moines, IA 50340-0835
(800) 223-3089
*to order the Royal Winton
"Welbeck" chintzware shown on
the book jacket, as well as a
number of tea accessories featured
in* Victoria *magazine*

**The Vintage Tea Shop at
Bergdorf Goodman**
754 Fifth Avenue
New York, NY 10019
(212) 753-7300
*vintage teapots, and everything
related to the service of tea*

Wedgwood
(800) 677-7860
fine china

Well-Sweep Herb Farm
205 Mount Bethel Road
Port Murray, NJ 07865
(908) 852-5390
herbal teas; mail order

Mark T. Wendell, Importer
50 Beharrel Street
West Concord, MA 01742
(978) 369-3709
*herbal and black teas, tea
accessories; mail order*

Windham Tea Club
12 Wilson Road
Windham, NH 03087
(800) 565-7527
tea-of-the-month club; mail order

Wolferman's
(800) 999-0169
www.wolferman's.com
*crumpets, muffins, other baked
goods; mail order*

Tea at the Windsor Hotel

Tea Salons

UNITED STATES & CANADA

Anglers & Writers
420 Hudson Street
New York, NY 10014
(212) 675-0810

Buckingham Bee
2179 Fourth Street
White Bear Lake, MN 55110
(651) 653-9533
also sells teas, tea accessories

Camellia Tearoom
828 First Street
Benicia, CA 94510
(707) 746-5293
also sells teas, tea accessories

Candlelight Inn Tearoom
30 Katharine Lee Bates Road
Falmouth, MA 01540
(508) 457-1177

Chai of Larkspur
25 Ward Street
Larkspur, CA 94939
(415) 945-7161
www.chaioflarkspur.com
also sells tea accessories, tea gifts

Chaiwalla Tearoom
1 Main Street
Salisbury, CT 06068
(860) 435-9758
also sells tea accessories

Chez Nous
723 Broadway East
Seattle, WA 98102
(206) 324-3711

Civil-La-Tea
39 York Street
Gettysburg, PA 17325
(717) 334-0992
www.cvn.net/~bhartman

The Devon Tearoom
294 Main Street
West Dennis, MA 02670
(508) 394-6068
www.devontearoom.com

The Dunbar Tea Shop
1 Water Street
Sandwich, MA 02563
(508) 833-2485

Elmwood Inn Tearoom
205 East Fourth Street
Perryville, KY 40468
(606) 332-2400

The Empress Hotel
721 Government Street
Victoria, B.C. V8W 1W5
Canada
(800) 441-1414; (250) 384-8111

English Ivy Tea Shoppe
10 Main Street
North Andover, MA 01845
(978) 683-6022

**The Four Seasons Hotels
with tea:**

BOSTON:
200 Boylston Street
Boston, MA 02116
(617) 351-2071

CHICAGO:
120 East Delaware Place
Chicago, IL 60611
(312) 280-8800

LOS ANGELES:
Four Seasons Beverly Hills
300 South Doheny Drive
Los Angeles, CA 90048
(310) 273-2222

NEW YORK:
57 East 57th Street
New York, NY 10022
(212) 758-5700

PHILADELPHIA:
1 Logan Square
Philadephia, PA 19103
(215) 963-1500

SEATTLE:
411 University Street
Seattle, WA 98101
(206) 621-1700

TORONTO:
21 Avenue Road
Toronto, ON M5R 2G1
(416) 964-0411

WASHINGTON, D.C.:
2800 Pennsylvania Avenue
Washington, D.C. 20007
(202) 342-0444

The Four Seasons Tearoom
75 North Baldwin Avenue
Sierra Madre, CA 91024
(626) 355-0045

Foxgloves
13 Church Street
Westfield, MA 01085
(413) 572-4899

The Front Parlour Tearoom
The British Shoppe
45 Wall Street
Madison, CT 06443
(203) 245-4521

The Gallery of Medina Tearoom
236 West Liberty Street
Medina, OH 44256
(800) 382-4180

Imperial Tea Court
1411 Powell Street
San Francisco, CA 94133
(415) 788-6080

The Johnson House
907 Route 228
Mars, PA 16046
(724) 625-2636

The Keeping Room
Barnhill's Bed & Breakfast
5347 Stewart Street
Milton, FL 32570
(850) 623-8412

Lady Mendl's Tea Salon
Inn at Irving Place
56 Irving Place
New York, NY 10003
(212) 533-4600

Lady Primrose's Tea Salon
500 Crescent Court
Dallas, TX 75201
(214) 871-8334

The Lipton Teahouse
124 East Colorado Boulevard
Pasadena, CA 91105
(626) 568-8787

MacNab's Tearoom
P.O. Box 206
Back River Road
Boothbay, ME 04537
(207) 633-7222; (800) 884-7222
also sells teas

Magnolia & Ivy at the Mansion
1402 Second Avenue
Columbus, GA 31901
(706) 317-4322

The Mark Hotel
25 East 77th Street
New York, NY 10021
(212) 744-4300

**McCharles House Restaurant
and Tearoom**
335 South C Street
Tustin, CA 92780
(714) 731-4063

Murchie's Tea & Coffee
5580 Parkwood Way
Richmond, B.C. V6V 2M4
Canada
(800) 663-0400

Olde English Tearoom
3 Devotion Road
Scotland, CT 06264
(860) 456-8651
by reservation only

Palm Court
The Plaza Hotel
Fifth Avenue at Central
Park South
New York, NY 10019
(212) 759-3000

Parlour Cafe at ABC Carpets
888 Broadway
New York, NY 10003
(212) 473-3000

Perennial Tearoom
1910 Post Alley
Seattle, WA 98101
(206) 448-4054

The Pierre Hotel
2 East 61st Street
New York, NY 10021
(212) 940-8195

**Queen Mary Confections &
Comestibles**
2912 NE 55th Street
Seattle, WA 98105
(206) 527-2770

The Ritz-Carlton Hotel
160 East Pearson Street
Chicago, IL 60611
(312) 573-5154

Rose Tree Cottage
828 East California Boulevard
Pasadena, CA 91106
(626) 793-3337
www.rosetreecottage.com
*also offers British gifts, teas,
and tours*

Serenity Tearoom
3305 Three Mile Road, NE
Grand Rapids, MI 49525
(616) 364-5640
www.celt4tea.com
also sells tea accessories; mail order

Someplace in Time Tearoom
132 South Glassell Street
Orange, CA 92866
(714) 538-9411
also sells tea accessories; mail order

Spicery Tearoom
7141 North 59th Avenue
Glendale, AZ 85301
(602) 937-6534

Sundial Gardens & Tearoom
59 Hidden Lake Road
Higganum, CT 06441
(860) 345-4290
www.chesterct.com/sundial

T Salon
11 East 20th Street
New York, NY 10003
(212) 398-0506
also sells tea accessories

The Tea Cozy
40 Bloomfield Avenue
Windsor, CT 06095
(860) 688-1450

Teaism
2009 R Street, NW
Washington, D.C. 20009
(888) 883-2476
also sells tea accessories

The Tearoom
7 East Broughton Street
Savannah, GA 31419
(912) 239-9690
also sells tea accessories

The Tea Shoppe
13 Steeple Street
Mashpee Commons
Mashpee, MA 02649
(508) 477-7261
also sells tea accessories

*Tea at the Charleston Tea
Plantation*

~ *The McCharles House
restaurant and tearoom*

Thistlefields
29 Chambersburg Street
Gettysburg, PA 17325
(717) 338-9131

Tohono Chul Park Tearoom
7366 North Paseo Del Norte
Tucson, AZ 85704
(520) 797-1222

Victorian Rose Tea Company, Ltd.
125 Mill Street
Occoquan, VA 22125
(703) 497-4795
also sells tea accessories; mail order

Victorian Rose Tearoom
619 Arnold Avenue
Point Pleasant Beach, NJ 08742
(732) 701-0900
also sells tea accessories

**Wild Myrtle Tearoom at Carolyn
& Company**
165 State Street
New London, CT 06320
(860) 447-3490

Windsor Court Hotel
300 Gravier Street
New Orleans, LA 70130
(800) 262-2662

Angelina
226 Rue de Rivoli
Paris 1ER
France
011-33-142 60 8200

The Four Seasons London
Hamilton Place, Park Lane
London W1A 1AZ
England
011-44-171 499 0888

Java, Java
26 Rupert Street
London W1V 7FN
England
011-44-171 734 5821

Mad Hatter's
28 Church Street
Launceston, Cornwall PL15 8AR
England
011-44-156 677 7188

Politico's
8 Artillery Row
Westminster, London SW1P 1RZ
England
011-44-171 828 0010

The Ritz
150 Piccadilly
London W1V 9DG
England
011-44-171 493 8181

Shepherds Tearooms
35 Little London
Chichester PO19 1PL
England
011-44-124 377 4761

Trinity House Tearoom
47 High Street
Manningtree, Essex
England
011-44-120 639 1410

Waterstone's Coffee Shop
Waterstone
4 Milsom Street
Bath BA1 1D5
England
011-44-122 544 4905

The Willow Rooms
217 Sauchiehall Street
Glasgow
Scotland
011-44-141 332 0521

The Windsor Hotel
103 Spring Street
Melbourne, Victoria 3000
Australia
011-61-39 633 3000

Tea Clubs, Organizations, Tours, and Museums

American Tea Masters Assoc.
41 Sutter Street, #1191
San Francisco, CA 94104
(415) 775-4227

**The Bramah Tea and Coffee
Museum**
The Clove Building
Maguire Street, Butlers Wharf
London SE1 2NQ
England
011-44-171 378 0222

The Charleston Tea Plantation
6617 May Bank Highway
Wadmalay Island, SC 29487
(800) 443-5987
retail shop and tours

**Exclusive Journeys Over
a Cuppa Tea**
P.O. Box 759
Willimantic, CT 06226
(860) 423-2344
tea tours to Britain and Europe

Pathfinder Travel
527 Belle Air
Carthage, MO 64836
(417) 358-2219
"Tea for Two" tour of England

Specialty World Travel
186 Alewife Brook Parkway
Cambridge, MA 02138
(800) 645-0001; (617) 476-1142
tea tours

The Tea Association of the USA
420 Lexington Avenue, Suite 825
New York, NY 10170
(212) 986-9415

Photo Credits

Recipe Index